D0021169

Butt Rot & Bottom Gas

Library of Congress Cataloging in Publication Number: 2007926711

ISBN: 978-1-59474-203-3
Printed in China

Typeset in Times and Helvetica

Designed by Bryn Ashburn
Illustrations by Jon Rogers

Distributed in North America by
Chronicle Books
680 Second Street
San Francisco, CA 94107

10 9 8 7 6 5 4 3 2

Quirk Books
215 Church Street
Philadelphia, PA 19106
www.quirkbooks.com

Butt Rot & Bottom Gas

A GLOSSARY OF TRAGICALLY MISUNDERSTOOD WORDS

BY ERIC GROVES, SR.

Introduction

The English language is full of misunderstood words.

Consider great tits. I adore great tits, especially when fully mature. I recently spent three weeks backpacking through Europe on a quest to photograph great tits in their natural environment. I returned home with hundreds of documentary photographs, all painstakingly labeled. Unfortunately, my work was confiscated at the airport by U.S. Customs; it seems that importing photographs of great tits is against the law.

Great tits is just one example of what I call a *pseudo-imprecation*—a word or term that sounds obscene but is not. Most birdwatchers know that great tits are charming and sprightly songbirds that live throughout Europe and Asia. But to the average American, the term *great tits* evokes a different connotation. And this ignorance comes with a hefty price tag.

Every year, pseudo-imprecations cause Americans to waste thousands of hours and millions of dollars. Stockbrokers who suggest that colleagues try naked shorting have been charged with sexual harassment. Farmers growing nipplefruit and horny goat weed have been investigated by the FBI. Some of our finest senior citizens have been sedated—or worse—simply for describing themselves as sexagenarians.

It is time to take a stand. It is time to set the record straight. From *arsole* and *bushmaster* to *cunt splice*, *dandy cock*, and beyond, *Butt Rot and Bottom Gas* gathers hundreds of misunderstood words and reveals their true meanings. Whenever possible, the definitions have been supplemented by an elucidating illustration or a famous quotation that uses the word in its proper context. Readers will also find a pronunciation key and a guide to symbols and abbreviations on the inside back cover.

If we work together, we can save hundreds of good, clean, eloquent words from needless desecration. The first step is to read this book carefully, study the definitions, and share them with your loved ones. The second step is to *use these words in casual conversation as often as possible.* Ask a waiter if his restaurant serves slippery dick. Ask a tourist if she speaks Anal. Celebrate the Feast of the Ass by inviting your friends and family to your home on January 14, and then spend the day snacking on butt roast and monkey nuts.

Through education and exposure, we can make a difference.

—Eric Groves, Sr.

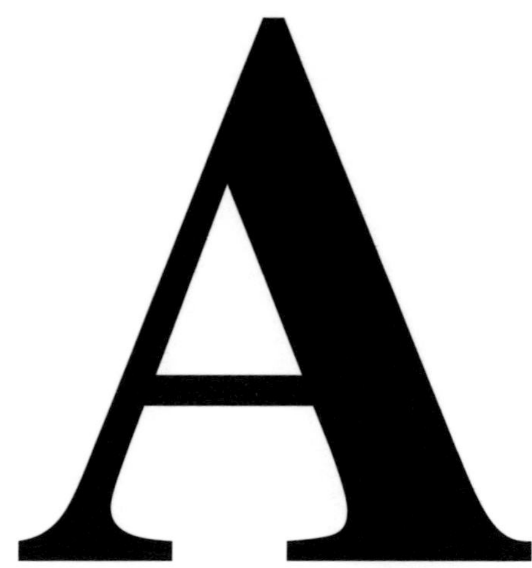

abreast /ə-brest′/ ***adj.*** shoulder to shoulder or side by side; ***also,*** to be knowledgeable about current events

abut /ə-bət′/ ***vb.*** to join together at a boundary

abut•ter /ə-bət′-ər/ ***n.*** one whose land abuts or joins the land of another

acock /ə-käk′/ ***adj.*** in a turned-up or tilted fashion, as with a hat

ad dam•num /ad-dam′-nəm/ ***n.*** the portion of a legal complaint in which a plaintiff states monetary damages

air cock /er käk/ ***n.*** a valve installed as part of the piping in the upper steam space of a boiler, allowing air into or out of the boiler; the valve opens when the boiler heats cold water and closes when the water is heated enough to become steam

ali•as dic•tus /ā′-lē-əs dik′-təs/ ***n.*** [Latin phrase meaning "another nomination" or "otherwise known as"] a fictitious name assumed by or given to a person for personal, professional, or criminal purposes

am•bush /am′-bûsh/ ***vb.*** to lie in wait and then attack

Anal /ä-näl′/ ***n.*** a Sino-Tibetan language spoken by several thousand members of the Naga tribe in southeast Manipur, India, and by other ethnic communities in Myanmar (formerly Burma) and Bangladesh; ***also known as*** Namfau

an•gi•na /an-jī′-nə/ ***n.*** [from the Greek word *ankhon*, meaning "strangling"] a potentially fatal disease caused when cholesterol-blocked arteries cut off oxygen to the heart, causing chest pains and respiratory distress—often an indicator of imminent myocardial infarction or heart attack, it should be treated immediately by a physician <History's most famous ***angina*** sufferer was Swedish industrialist Alfred Nobel (1833–1896). Nobel was the inventor of nitroglycerin, a substance that, ironically, was later found to be an effective treatment for angina.>

an•i•ma•lia /a-nə-mä′-lyə/ ***n.*** the kingdom of terrestrial life that includes all animals

an•nu•al as•say /an′-yü-əl a-sā′/ ***n.*** a nationwide annual test of gold to ascertain adherence to standards of weight and purity

an•nul /ə-nəl′/ ***vb.*** to cancel or make void, as for a marriage

an•nu•lus /an′-yə-ləs/ ***n.*** [from the Latin word *annus*, meaning "a rounding"] a ring or anything ring shaped; in geometry, a solid shape encircling a straight-line axis (in other words, a doughnut)

ap•ple of Sod•om /a′-pəl əv sä′-dəm/ ***n.*** a spiny greenish gray plant native to the Jordan River valley and Dead Sea regions of Israel

ar•rears /ə-rirz′/ ***n.*** money that is due and payable but has not been paid; ***also***, a job that needs to be finished but remains unfinished

> "Observation is so wide awake, and facts are being so rapidly added to the sum of human experience, that it appears as if the theorizer would always be in arrears, and were doomed forever to arrive at imperfect conclusions."
>
> —Henry David Thoreau, "A Week on the Concord and Merrimac Rivers"

ar•sole /är′-sōl/ ***n.*** an organic chemical compound identified by the chemical formula C_4H_5As—similar to a pyrrole, or a heterocyclic aromatic organic compound, but much less aromatic and containing an arsenic atom instead of a nitrogen atom

as•i•nine /a′-sə-nīn/ ***adj.*** having stupid, silly, and stubborn traits usually associated with donkeys, burros, and other asses; ***also***, anyone or anything idiotic, moronic, etc.

as•por•ta•tion /as-pôr-tā′-shən/ ***n.*** the removal of things from one place to another

ASS ***abbr.*** the acronym for the chemical argininosuccinate synthetase

as•sag•ai /as′-ə-gī/ ***n.*** a spear with a wooden shaft and an elongated metal tip, used in South Africa—probably derived from the African tree of the same name whose wood was considered ideal for spear-making by Bantu warriors

assagai

> "A birdchief bluestreaked and feathered in war panoply with his assagai, striding through a crackling canebrake over beechmast and acorns."
>
> —JAMES JOYCE, *ULYSSES*

As•sam /ə-sam′/ ***n.*** a type of black tea, of Indian origin, having a rich malt flavor

as•sart /ə-särt′/ ***n.*** land that has been substantially cleared of bushes and trees

as•say /a-sā′/ ***vb.*** an analysis of a metal, drug, etc., to determine the identity and purity of ingredients

as•sent /ə-sent′/ ***n.*** compliance or agreement; an approval of something

as•set-cov•er•age test /a′-set-kəv′-rij test/ ***n.*** a limitation on bond indentures in accounting

as•set strip•ping /a′-set strip′-iŋ/ ***vb.*** to seek profit by buying a company and selling its assets

as•set turn•over /a′-set tərn′-ō-vər/ ***n.*** a measure of how efficiently a business's assets are used to produce sales

as•si•ette /a-sē-et′/ ***n.*** a selection of cold meats served on a plate

as•sign•or /a-sə-nor′/ ***n.*** a person or entity who assigns or transfers property to another person or entity

as•siz•es /ə-sīz′-əz/ ***n.*** British judges who, during medieval times, traveled a route or circuit through designated Assize towns to hear criminal cases and render verdicts; abolished by the Courts Act of 1971 in favor of the Crown Court, which now handles criminal trials and appeals throughout Britain

as•so•nance /a′-sə-nəns/ ***n.*** the deliberate repetition of vowel sounds in a sentence

as•swage /ə-swāj′/ ***vb.*** to satisfy someone or calm a person; variant spelling of ***assuage***

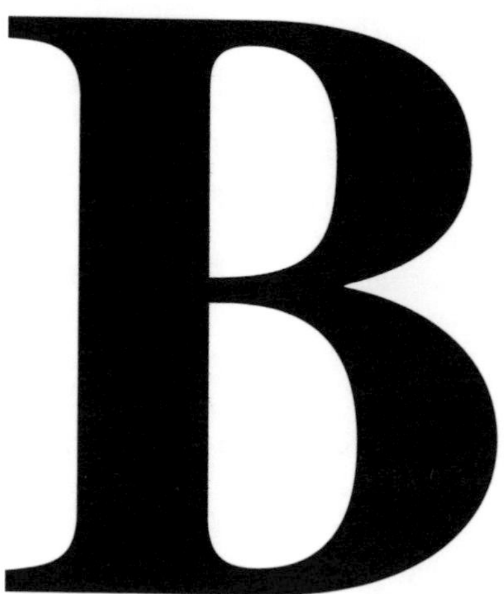

back•hoe /bak′-hō/ ***n.*** a hydraulically powered digging machine with a metal bucket attached to an articulated mechanical arm that removes large amounts of soil to create large trenches and excavated spaces for foundations, septic systems, etc.

bag•asse /bə-gas′/ ***n.*** [From the French *bagasse* and the Spanish *bagazo*, meaning "pulp"] the refuse remaining after sugarcane is pulped to produce sugar <Crushed ***bagasse*** is a renewable biofuel routinely burned in sugar mills to generate electricity and to power machinery.>

bag•ging /ba′-giŋ/ ***n.*** fabric used to make bags

ball change /bôl chānj/ ***n.*** two-step movement used in a variety of dances, in which the performer shifts a portion of his or her weight onto the ball of one foot, then follows with a step on the opposite foot (often counted in a snappy manner, "A-one and a-two and a-three," etc.) <COMBINED USAGE **kick ball change** a dancer kicks before executing the ball change; **heel ball change** a dancer touches the heel to the floor before the ball change>

ball cock /bôl käk/ ***n.*** a valve attached to a floating ball, which opens the valve when elevated; most commonly used in flush toilets

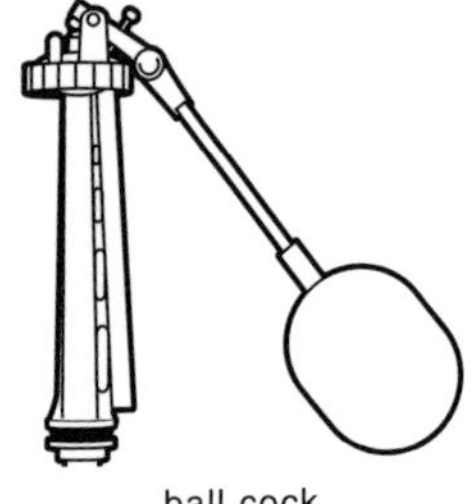
ball cock

ball•er /bô′-lər/ ***n.*** a player in basketball, tennis, or paintball—in basketball, one who scores aggressively for the team; in tennis, one who has a powerful swing; in paintball, any participant

ball-in-hand /bôl-in-hand′/ ***n.*** the occurrence in billiards or pool of a player placing the cue ball anywhere on the playing table and hitting any ball desired; typically occurs after an opponent has committed a foul (such as scratching the table)

bal•lis•tic en•try /bə-lis′-tik en′-trē/ ***n.*** a type of entrance that occurs when a vehicle (or spacecraft) entering a planet's atmosphere uses only drag or air friction to reduce speed—contrasts with spacecraft that use aerodynamic lift, or the directing of airflow downward <The manned *Mercury* spacecrafts (1959–63) were ***ballistic entry*** vehicles, whereas the winged space shuttle (1981–present) is an aerodynamic lift entry vehicle.>

ball mill /bôl mil/ ***n.*** a pulverizing machine used in industry to reduce materials such as ceramics, ores, etc., into fine powder; consists of a horizontal cylinder filled with steel or ceramic balls that rotates mechanically on its axis and can grind materials to tolerances of ten-thousandths of a millimeter; ***also***, a device used to mix materials such as paints and chemicals

ball out /bôl aût/ ***n.*** in water-polo, a call for a ball to be thrown to the referee

ball-peen ham•mer /bôl′-pēn ham′-ər/ ***n.*** a hammer with a rounded head used for shaping and forming sheet metal; commonly used to repair damaged automobile parts such as fenders

ball whisk /bôl wisk/ ***n.*** a kitchen utensil often used to whip eggs

ban•ger /baŋ′-ər/ ***n.*** an English sausage made with pork meat

bare•back /bār′-bak/ ***adv. or adj.*** a type of horseback riding without the use of a saddle

BARF ***abbr.*** the acronym for Biologically Appropriate Raw Food, a term used in the pet-food industry

bar•fi /bär′-fē/ ***n.*** a sweet, cheesecake-like dessert, popular in India and Pakistan, made with condensed milk, mangoes, cashews, and often a bit of edible silver leaf

bas•tar•da /bä-stär′-də/ ***n., often cap.*** [From the Italian *bastarda*, "bastard" (akin to "not quite genuine")] an elegant font or typeface used in France and Germany in the 1300s and 1400s that was a hybrid of earlier scripts and a simplified version of more elaborate Gothic scripts—often used in the hand copying of books deemed to be of lesser significance than the Bible or other religious treatises

bas•tar•dane /bas′-tər-dān/ ***n.*** an alternative term for ethano-bridged noradamante, a chemical compound similar in composition, odor, and appearance to adamantane, a crystalline chemical compound <The chemical structure of ***bastardane*** contains a unique ethanol bridge, or connection between molecules, which differentiates it from other hydrocarbons (chemical compounds made of hydrogen and carbon); bastardane gets its name from the fact that its ethano-bridge varies from ordinary hydrocarbons, making it an irregular compound.>

bas•tard sword /bas′-tərd sō(ə)rd/ ***n.*** a type of sword used in Europe from about 1350 to 1550; almost a true longsword, it is a hybrid between a longsword (two-handed sword about 4 feet long) and a shorter one-handed arming sword, about 2–3 feet long

ba•tarde /bä-tärd′/ ***n.*** a French sauce made with butter and egg yolks

Bath bun /bath bən/ ***n.*** a type of yeast bread, colored with saffron, that originated in the city of Bath, England

beat around the bush /bēt ə-raônd′ thə bəsh/ ***vb. phrase*** to delay, procrastinate; to fail to get to the point

bea•ver /bē′-vər/ ***n.*** a land-dwelling and an aquatic mammal, a member of the order Rodentia and one of the largest rodents on Earth, weighing an average 55 pounds <Characterized by sleek brown fur and wide tails, ***beavers*** abound in forests throughout North America and are known for building dams and lodges or hutlike shelters across streams and rivers, creating beneficial wetlands.>

bea•ver hat /bē′-vər hat/ ***n.*** a type of hat made from beaver pelts that was popular in Europe from 1550 to 1850; the hat was prized for its softness and durability <Demand for pelts to make ***beaver hats*** caused a temporary disappearance of the beaver in western Europe.>

> "On the top of the Crumpetty Tree
> The Quangle Wangle sat,
> But his face you could not see,
> On account of his Beaver Hat."
>
> —Edward Lear, "The Quangle Wangle's Hat"

bed•fel•low /bed′-fel-ō/ ***n.*** an ally or friend

bed•hug /bed′-həg/ ***n.*** an Indonesian drum used in traditional musical performances

bed load /bed lōd/ ***n.*** particles of gravel carried along a streambed by the current

beef•eat•ers /bē′-fēt-ərz/ ***n., often cap.*** the 36 royal guards of the Tower of London, a large castle built along London's Thames River; also called the Yeoman Warders of Her Majesty's Royal Palace and Fortress, the Tower of London <The name ***Beefeaters*** probably came from the large ration of beef given to the guards as partial payment for the performance of their royal duties. For most of their history, dating back to the 1300s, the Beefeaters guarded prisoners in the tower; today they escort approximately 1.3 million visitors annually to view the famed British Crown Jewels, which are stored in the tower.>

beef•wood /bēf′-wûd/ ***n.*** a pinelike tree native to Australia

be•tween a rock and a hard place /bi-twēn′ ə räk ənd ə härd plās/ ***prep. phrase*** to be in a difficult predicament that offers only unpleasant options for getting out

BFOQ /bē′-fək/ ***abbr.*** the acronym for Bona Fide Occupational Qualification—or a legitimate job requirement—as described in the United States Code of Federal Regulations, title 20, volume 3, chapter 5, part 651, section 651.10. <A ***BFOQ*** is an exception to the general prohibition against employment discrimination based on age, disability, gender, race, etc., because it may, in certain cases, prevent individuals from physically performing a job. Therefore, the federal Equal Employment Opportunity

Commission must determine that the BFOQ is legitimate and not simply a ruse to prevent select individuals from gaining a particular job.>

bil•ly•cock /bil′-ē-käk/ ***n.*** a derby hat

bis•sext•ile /bī-seks′-tīl/ ***adj.*** [From the Latin word *bissextus*, meaning “two sixes” and referring to ancient Roman leap-year calendars in which two consecutive days were dated March 6] a leap year, or a year with an extra day added to maintain accuracy <Because a solar year consists of 365¼ days, our calendar would be inaccurate if it maintained the same number of days each year. By alternately adding an extra, or intercalating, day to February, accuracy is maintained.>

black•ball /blak′-bôl/ ***n.*** a vote against someone or something that is taken or assumed in a secret or underhanded manner

black•cock /blak′-käk/ ***n.*** in the black grouse family of birds, the male of the species

blo•vi•ate /blō′-vē-āt/ ***vb.*** to speak for quite a while in a pompous manner

blow•ball /blō′-bôl/ ***n.*** an herb of the genus *Taraxacum* having bright yellow flowers

blow•fish /blō′-fish/ ***n.*** a type of fish; ***also called*** pufferfish

blow•hard /blō′-härd/ ***n.*** an obnoxious braggart

blow•hole /blō′-hōl/ ***n.*** a nostril-like opening in the heads of cetaceans such as whales and dolphins

blow valve /blō valv/ ***n.*** a valve in one of the cylinders of a steam engine

blow your own horn /blō′ yər ōn hô(ə)rn/ ***vb. phrase*** to boast about oneself

blue ball /blü bôl/ ***n.*** a blue-colored ball worth five points that is used in snooker, a type of billiard game

blue pet•er /blü pē′-tər/ ***n.*** a nautical signal flag, with a white square centered on a blue field, hoisted by a docked ship to indicate a readiness to get under way

blue suck•er /blü sək′-ər/ ***n.*** a species of freshwater fish

blue tit /blü tit/ ***n.*** a member of the family Paridae (***also called*** tits) and a small tree-perching songbird with an attractive blue crest, wings, and tail that is found throughout forests in Europe and Asia; ***also called*** *Parus caeruleus* <The ***blue tit*** has always been popular among bird watchers due to its lively antics while feeding on wild nuts and its shrieking, "Tee, tee, tee!">

bon•er /bō′-nər/ ***n.*** a kitchen knife used to remove bones from meat and poultry

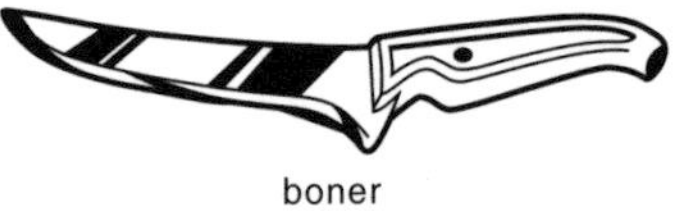

boner

bon•i•fi•ca•tion /bō-ni-fi-kā′-shən/ ***n.*** the remission or waiver of a tax, particularly on export goods

boo•by prize /bü′-bē prīz/ ***n.*** a fun prize given to the worst player in a silly game

boo•ty /bü′-tē/ ***n.*** treasure or prizes, usually stolen or illicit

> "All politics is a matter of working hard without reward, or with a living wage for a time, in the hope of booty later."
>
> —Ernest Hemingway, "Old Newsman Writes: A Letter from Cuba"

bot•tom ash /bä′-təm ash/ ***n.*** the nonburning components of coal

bot•tom gas /bä′-təm gas/ ***n.*** a type of breathing gas carried in portable tanks and inhaled by under-water divers

bot•tom-hole con•tract /bä′-təm-hōl kän′-trakt/ ***n.*** a type of oil-drilling contract in which the landowner pays the lessee

bot•tom•ry /bä′-təm-rē/ ***n.*** a type of contract in which a shipowner offers his or her vessel as collateral to obtain a loan to fund an expedition

brain fag /brān fag/ ***n.*** the state that occurs when a person psychologically disrupts his or her bodily functions

brass balls /brass bôlz/ ***n.*** parts used in the rotor assemblies of helicopters

Bra•zil nuts /brə-zil′ nətz/ ***n.*** hard-shelled, oily, three-sided nuts that grow in clusters on the *Bertholletia excelsa* tree, found in South America

breast-deep /brest′-dēp/ ***adj.*** up to one's breast, that is, the chest; chest high

breast•hook /brest′-hûk/ ***n.*** a thick piece of wood placed across the stern (rear) of a ship

breast•plate /brest′-plāt/ ***n.*** the piece that covers the chest in a suit of armor

brown ball /braûn bôl/ ***n.*** a brown-colored ball worth four points; used in snooker, a type of billiard game

bug•ger /bəg′-ər/ ***n.*** a person who secretly installs electronic listening devices

bulb bast•er /bəlb bāst′-ər/ ***n.*** a kitchen utensil that assists with basting, or moistening, meat during cooking

bulge the on•ion bag /bəlj thə ən′-yən bag/ ***vb. phrase*** British slang for scoring a goal in soccer (or football, as it's known in Great Britain) <The term ***bulge the onion bag*** refers to the resemblance between the soccer nets and the net bags in which onions are sold.>

bung•hole /buŋ′-hōl/ ***n.*** a hole in a wooden barrel that releases liquid; the hole is plugged with a cork called a bung

> "To what base uses we may return, Horatio! Why may not imagination trace the noble dust of Alexander, till he find it stopping a bunghole?"
>
> —William Shakespeare, *Hamlet*

bun•ya nut /bən′-yə nət/ ***n.*** a variety of nut that grows on the Australian pine tree *Araucaria bidwilli*

bush•el /bûsh′-əl/ ***n.*** a dry measure for produce or grain that contains 4 pecks, or 8 gallons, or 32 quarts

bush•man /bûsh′-mən/ ***n.*** a person (typically a backwoodsman) who dwells in the Australian bush

bush•mas•ter /bûsh′-mas-tər/ ***n.*** a large venomous snake found in Central and South America

bush•meat /bûsh′-mēt/ ***n.*** small animals such as rats and monkeys that are hunted for sustenance in forests and jungles, when larger game animals are not readily available

bush•whack /bûsh′-wak/ ***vb.*** to ambush or engage in a surprise or guerilla attack

bus•tard /bəs′-tərd/ ***n.*** any of the large-bodied birds of the family Otididae

but•ter•nut /bə′-tər-nət/ ***n.*** a North American walnut tree, the *Juglans cinerea*

butt hinge /bət hinj/ ***n.*** a hinge partially recessed into a door's edge

butt joint /bət joint/ ***n.*** a joint made by placing two pieces of material end-to-side or end-to-end

butt log /bət lôg/ ***n.*** in logging, the largest section of a tree that is sawn off near the tree's stump, or butt

Butt Re•port /bət ri-pôrt′/ ***n.*** a comprehensive World War II document prepared for British Prime Minister Winston Churchill by his trusted friend D. M. Butt of the British War Cabinet Secretariat that shocked the British government with the revelation that 33 percent of Royal Air Force Bomber Command planes were routinely failing to drop their loads on their designated targets; the information stirred rapid advances in bomb-sight technology as well as improvements in bombing strategies and tactics, all of which contributed to the Allied victory in 1945

but•tress /bə′-trəs/ ***n.*** a stone or brick structure built to hold up a wall

butt roast /bət rōst/ ***n.*** a cut of meat that comes from a pig's shoulder <A ***butt roast*** is typically roasted or barbecued; if barbecued, the butt is often prepared before cooking with a commercially prepared dry-rub mixture of seasonings. Butt rubbing should be done carefully to bring out the meat's maximum flavor.>

butt rot /bət rät/ ***n.*** a fungal disease affecting the butt, or base, of a tree

butt rot

butt shaft /bət shaft/ ***n.*** an arrow with a blunt or unsharpened tip

"Cupid's butt-shaft is too hard for Hercules' club, and therefore too much odds for a Spaniard's rapier."

—William Shakespeare, *Love's Labour's Lost*

butt weld /bət weld/ ***n.*** a weld made by joining together the flat ends of sheet metal

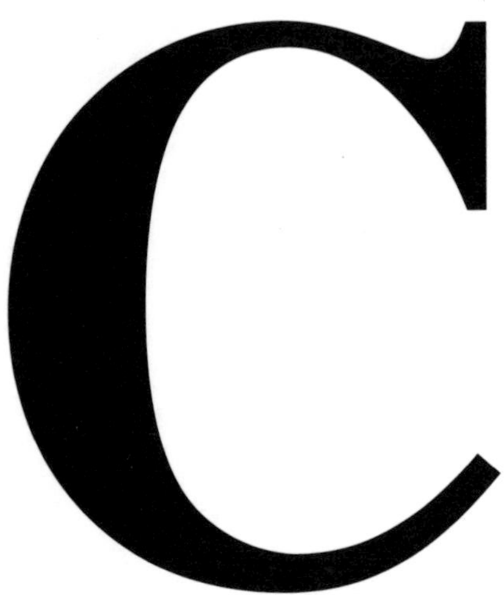

ca•cao /kə-kaû′/ ***n.*** a tropical South American tree, *Theobroma cacao*, that produces cacao or cocoa beans

can•dy•tuft /kan′-dē-təft/ ***n.*** a genus of low-growing plants characterized by multicolored blooms

cas•tel•lat•ed /kas-tə-lā′-təd/ ***adj.*** decorated with battlements to resemble a castle

cham•ber busi•ness /chām′-bər biz′-nəs/ ***n.*** official business conducted by a judge in chambers

cher•ry pick•ing /cher′-ē pi′-kiŋ/ ***vb.*** to select only the information that supports one's opinion

chick sex•ing /chik seks′-iŋ/ ***n.*** the process used by biologists and other animal handlers to determine the gender of newly hatched chicks <The most common method of ***chick sexing***, called vent sexing, involves squeezing the chick's posterior to reveal its genitals. This method was first introduced to the West in 1933 by two Japanese professors in their seminal book, *Sexing Baby Chicks*.>

cir•cum•scribe /sər-kəm-skrīb′/ ***vb.*** to draw a circle around something

clam•at•or•i•al /klam-ə-tôr′-ē-əl/ ***adj.*** of or relating to the clamatores, a diverse group of tree-perching song-birds with limited musical ability

clam•bake /klam′-bāk/ ***n.*** a meal generally prepared near the ocean and featuring clams and other shellfish

cleav•age /klē′-vij/ ***n.*** the propensity of crystalline minerals to break along weak planes, exposing mirror-like facets <The principle of ***cleavage*** is employed by gemstone cutters, who use precision strikes to create multifaceted gemstones. In the electronics industry, thin wafers of silicon, a commonly occurring crystal, are carefully cleaved to create transistors, semiconductors, solar cells, etc.>

cleav•age fur•row /klē′-vij fər′-ō/ ***n.*** the constriction of an animal-cell membrane that typically begins cytokinesis, the process of cell division whereby one cell splits into two, two split into four, and so forth

cli•max com•mu•ni•ty /klī′-maks kə-myü′-nə-tē/ ***n.*** in ecology, a mature, stabilized community of animals and vegetation that is well adapted to a specific environment <The American botanist Frederic Clements (1874–1945) disseminated the idea of the ***climax community*** during the early twentieth century. His ideas have since fallen out of favor among botanists, ecologists, and others because ecological disruptions tend to occur so frequently that apparent stability is probably illusory or temporary. However, a minority of scientists still refer to old-growth forests as climaxes.>

cli•to•rin /klī-tôr′-in/ ***n.*** a chemical compound found in the leaves of the South American plants *Trillium undulatum* and *Acalypha indicia*

coc•co•lite /käk′-ə-līt/ ***n.*** the archaic name for a white and green crystalline gemstone, now called diopside, often sought because its discovery in mining digs can indicate the presence of diamonds

coc•cyx /käk′-siks/ ***n.*** [From the Latin word *coccyges*, meaning "cuckoo"] the last bone of the spinal column or backbone; ***also called*** tailbone <The ***coccyx*** vaguely resembles the beak of a cuckoo bird, hence the term. It appears to be vestigial, or left over, from an earlier evolutionary era and is substantially nonfunctional; nevertheless, care must be taken not to injure or break it because doing so can result in intense pain and a lengthy recuperation.>

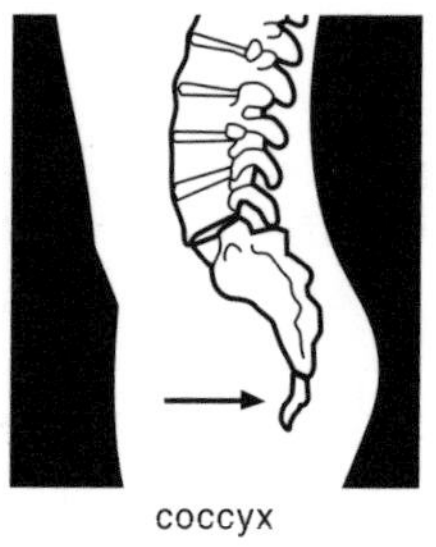
coccyx

co•chlea /käk′-lē-ə/ ***n.*** [From the Latin word *coclea*, meaning "snail"] the spiral structure inside the inner ear that is filled with fluid and fine hairs that transmit auditory signals to the brain

cock•ade /käk′-ād/ ***n.*** a ribbon or other decoration worn as a badge, usually on a hat

cock and bull sto•ry /käk ənd bəl stôr′-ē/ ***n.*** a story or excuse that is very hard to believe

cock•a•poo /käk′-ə-pü/ ***n.*** a dog that is a cross between a poodle and a cocker spaniel

cock•boat /käk′-bōt/ ***n.*** a small boat that is moved forward by the use of paddles

cock•chaf•er /käk′-chā-fər/ ***n.*** a large European beetle of the family Scarabaedaeidae that feeds on crops and plant roots; ***also known as*** maybug <The ***cockchafer***'s voracious appetite and destructive propensities prompted a twentieth-century extermination program that virtually eradicated the insect throughout Europe. But, as pesticide use has become more strictly regulated worldwide, the cockchafer has staged a modest comeback.>

cock horse /käk hôrs/ ***n.*** a child's toy, either a rocking horse or a long pole with a fanciful horse's head at one end

cock•le /kä′-k^{ə}l/ ***n.*** a small marine mollusk related to the oyster

cock•mast•er /käk′-mas-tər/ ***n.*** a person who breeds roosters for fighting

cock-of-the-rock /käk′-əv-thə-räk/ ***n.*** a South American bird of the genus *Rupicola*

cock•pit /käk′-pit/ ***n.*** an enclosed space in an airplane where a pilot sits

cock•shy /käk′-shī/ ***n.*** the tossing of an object at a target in any game that tests the accuracy of contestants' throwing skills <The term ***cockshy*** may derive from an ancient sport in which sticks were hurled at live cocks, or chickens.>

com•mode /kə-mōd′/ ***n.*** an ornate women's cap popular in the seventeenth and eighteenth centuries

con•di•ment /kän′-də-mənt/ ***n.*** something poured or spread over food to improve the taste

con fu•o•co /kôn fü-ō′-kō/ ***adv.*** or ***adj.*** [An Italian phrase meaning "with fire"] a musical term meaning "in a spirited manner"

con•gen•i•tal /kən-je′-nə-t^{ə}l/ ***adj.*** a type of physiological abnormality or defect apparent at birth, as opposed to a medical condition acquired through illness or injury after birth <***Congenital*** birth defects may be caused by trauma to the womb, nutritional imbalances, inherited genetic factors, environmental factors, or unknown causes. They occur in 2–3 percent of babies. A congenital disorder may range from a harmless birthmark to more serious conditions such as missing limbs.>

cop•u•la /kä′-pyə-lə/ ***n.*** in English grammar, a connection between the subject part of a sentence and the predicate part of a sentence; these are generally forms of the verb “to be”

cou•pling /kə′-pliŋ/ ***n.*** in plumbing, a fitting that joins two pieces of pipe

cow•lick /kaû′-lik/ ***n.*** a lock of hair that sticks up, refusing to lie flat

cow•pea /kaû′-pē/ ***n.*** an Asian legume, *Vigna unguiculata*; ***also called*** black-eyed pea

crack spread /krak spred/ ***n.*** a method used in commodities exchanges (marketplaces such as the Chicago Board of Trade) whereby raw products, including crude oil, are bought, sold, and traded <In this sense, to *crack* means to refine crude oil into more valuable heating oil and gasoline, and a *spread* is the difference between two amounts of money. Therefore, a ***crack spread*** is the strategy of buying oil futures (contracts allowing one to buy or sell oil at a fixed price in the future) and later, when the oil is refined, selling the futures in heating oil and gasoline.>

cram•down /kram′-daûn/ ***n.*** a bankruptcy court’s acceptance of a debtor’s repayment terms, despite the objections of creditors

CRAP ***abbr.*** the former acronym for the Canadian Reform Alliance Party; now known as the Canadian Alliance

crap•i•non /kra′-pi-nän/ ***n.*** a chemical compound that can be used therapeutically as an anticholinergic, or medicine that mitigates the side effects of acetylcholine, an organic compound synthesized to treat Alzheimer's disease <Because acetylcholine can produce side effects such as constipation, ***crapinon*** and other anticholinergics are useful for their ability to hinder such undesirable reactions.>

cream•ing ma•chine /krē′-miŋ mə′-shēn/ ***n.*** an assembly-line machine used to deposit fat-based cream fillings from one or more metal creaming heads into various types of cookies

cream nut /krēm nət/ ***n.*** another name for a Brazil nut, a hard-shelled, oily, three-sided nut that grows in clusters on the *Bertholletia excelsa* tree in South America

cream sauce /krēm sôs/ ***n.*** a sauce made of flour, butter, and cream

cream wave /krēm wāv/ ***n.*** a large gray-white moth

cris•py shrimp balls /kris′-pē shrimp bôlz/ ***n.*** appetizers made with shrimp and water chestnuts

crotch•ety /krä′-chə-tē/ ***adj.*** hard to get along with; cantankerous

cui•rass /kwi-ras′/ ***n.*** the breastplate in a suit of armor

cum all /kəm ôl/ ***vb.*** to pay share buyers every advantage of their shares

cum div•i•dend /kəm di′-və-dend/ ***n.*** a payment received by share buyers if a stock is sold

cum•ene /kyü′-mēn/ ***n.*** a standard organic solvent having a strong odor

cum file /kyüm fīl/ ***n.*** a student's cumulative academic record

cum•mer /kə′-mər/ ***n.*** [From the medieval French word *commère*, meaning "companion mother"] an alternative term for a godmother, or a woman chosen by parents to care for their children if the parents die

cum•ming•to•nite /kə′-miŋ-tə-nīt/ ***n.*** a translucent green iron-bearing mineral; ***also known as*** magnesium iron silicate hydroxide <***Cummingtonite*** was discovered in 1824 near the town of Cummington, Massachusetts. The mineral also occurs in Great Britain, South Africa, and Sweden.>

cum•quat /kəm′-kwät/ ***n.*** a small, orange citrus fruit; variant spelling of ***kumquat***

cum rights /kyüm rīts/ ***n.*** rights sold along with shares of existing stock so that the buyer may purchase a new issue, or stock that will be sold for the first time to raise capital for a new venture

cum tes•ta•men•to an•ne•xo /kəm tes′-tə-men-tō -ə-neks′-ō/ ***prep. phrase.*** [Latin phrase] a term used in probate law that means “with the Will annexed”

cunc•ta•tor /kəŋk′-tā-tər/ ***n.*** a person who procrastinates, delays, or wastes time

cunt•line /kənt′-līn/ ***n.*** the valley, or depression, between each of the strands of a rope or cable

cunt splice /kənt splīs/ ***n.*** a type of rope splice in which two ropes, or two parts of a single rope, are tied together by unraveling strands and then interweaving them <Rope splices are generally used by sailors to make an eye or loop in a rope. A ***cunt splice*** is used when an extremely strong knot is required or when the rope eye needs to close tightly when tension is applied.>

cunt splice

> “Well . . . a simple thing like a cunt splice will not take a man-of-war’s bosom long, I believe.”
>
> —Patrick O’Brien, *Master and Commander*

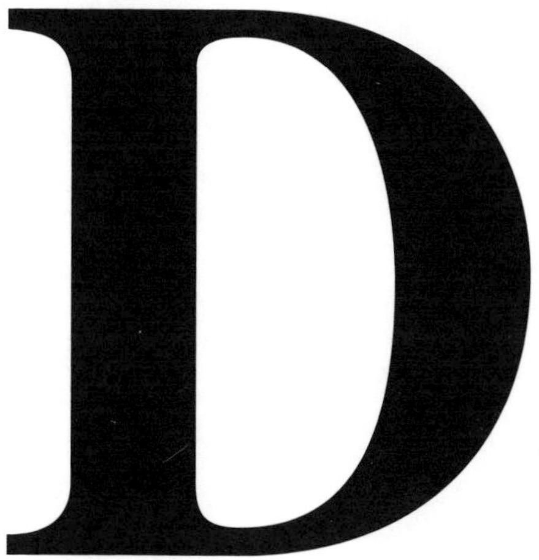

dai•fu•ku /dī′-fü-kü/ ***n.*** a Japanese dessert consisting of rice cakes and bean paste

dam /dam/ ***n.*** a wall, often made of concrete, used to hold back water

dam•mer /da′-mər/ ***n.*** a type of resin tapped from Australian trees of the genus *Agathis*

DAMN ***abbr.*** the acronym for the molecule diamino-maleonitrile, a highly toxic polymer of hydrogen cyanide

dam•ni•fy /dam′-nə-fī/ ***n.*** to cause damage or injurious loss

dandy cock

dan•dy cock /dan′-dē käk/ ***n.*** a member of any of several miniature breeds of chickens that are about one-fourth the size of common breeds <***Dandy cock*** roosters are generally shown at fairs and competitions or even kept as household pets, whereas dandy cock hens are often used for egg laying.>

das•tard /das′-tərd/ ***n.*** a cowardly bad guy

date of cleav•age /dāt əv klē′-vij/ ***n.*** the date of filing a voluntary petition of bankruptcy

dead ball /ded bôl/ ***n.*** in American football, a ball that a referee has ruled as no longer in play, either because the player carrying the ball has run out of bounds (past the marked lines of the field's edges) or is tackled; teams may neither take possession of the ball nor call any plays until the referee rules that play has officially resumed

de•cock•er /dē-kä′-kər/ ***n.*** the part of a pistol that allows the hammer to be safely lowered

de•coc•tion /di-käk′-shən/ ***n.*** an extract procured by boiling away a material to obtain its pure flavor or essence

> "His duty he always faithfully did; but duty is sometimes a dry obligation, and he was for irrigating its aridity, whensoever possible, with a fertilizing decoction of strong waters."
>
> —HERMAN MELVILLE, *BILLY BUDD*

deep holes /dēp hōlz/ ***n.*** in factory machining, holes drilled into various materials by professional machinists using industrial-quality drill presses in which each hole's diameter-to-depth ratio is 1 to 5 or greater (for example, a hole that is one inch wide and five inches deep)

dick•er /di′-kər/ ***vb.*** to engage in petty haggling or negotiating

dick•ey /di′-kē/ ***n.*** on men, a fake shirtfront; on women, a fake blouse front

dick•ite /di′-kīt/ ***n.*** a claylike mineral with micalike layers of silicate sheets

Dick test /dik test/ ***n.*** a procedure developed in 1924 by the American bacteriologist Dr. George Frederick Dick (1881–1967) and his wife, Gladys Rowena (1881–1963), to test for the presence of scarlet fever <Dr. Dick began his seminal medical studies in the Army Medical Corps during World War I; they culminated in his climactic discovery of the Streptococcus bacterial toxins that produce scarlet fever.>

dic•ta /dik′-tə/ ***n.*** the opinions of a judge that go beyond the principal issues or facts of a case

dik-dik /dik′-dik/ ***n.*** a member of the genus *Madoqua*; a small brown and white antelope roaming the bushlands of eastern Africa, it has large beautiful ears and stubby striated horns <The ***dik-dik***'s name comes from the cry it emits when frightened or disturbed.>

dike /dīk/ ***n.*** [from the Dutch word *dijk*, meaning "earthen dam"] a wall made of tons of compacted soil and rubble used to hold back bodies of water to prevent flooding of nearby inhabited lowlands <The first known earthen ***dikes*** were built in India around 2600 BC by the Harappan civilization; currently, the world's longest dike is the Saemangeum Seawall in South Korea.>

dik•kops /di′-kəps/ ***n.*** a South African bird

dir•ty blonde /dər′-tē bländ/ ***adj.*** a description for hair (usually a woman's) that is dark blonde mixed with brown

dong /dôŋ/ ***n.*** the official currency of Vietnam

dou•ble-slit ex•per•i•ment /də′-bəl-slit ik-sper′-ə-mənt/ ***n.*** an experiment first performed in 1805 by the British physicist Thomas Young (1773–1829) to test whether light was "corpuscular," meaning composed of particles, or composed of waves similar to sound waves; Young allowed sunlight to shine through two slits in an opaque barrier and then studied the patterns produced on a screen to gather his scientific data

dou•ble tonguing /də′-bəl təŋ′-iŋ/ ***n.*** a musical technique in which players of wind or brass instruments silently and repeatedly pronounce "too-kuh" while blowing their instruments, producing notes in rapid succession

drip dick•ey /drip di′-kē/ ***n.*** a disposable fabric collar that slips over the mouth of a wine bottle and soaks up drips that might otherwise discolor clothing or tablecloths

ear•jack•ing /ir-ja′-kiŋ/ ***vb.*** to eavesdrop on a private conversation

egg cream /eg krēm/ ***n.*** a New York drink made of chocolate syrup, milk, and seltzer

ejac•u•late /i-ja′-kyə-lāt/ ***vb.*** to make a loud, sudden yell or pronouncement

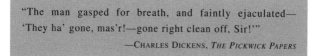

> "The man gasped for breath, and faintly ejaculated—'They ha' gone, mas'r!—gone right clean off, Sir!'"
>
> —Charles Dickens, *The Pickwick Papers*

ejec•tum /i-jek′-təm/ ***n.*** matter thrown onto land by the sea

em•purp•le /im-pər′-pəl/ ***vb.*** to cause something to become purple

en•clit•ic /en-kli′-tik/ ***adj.*** in grammar, a type of word that depends on a preceding word for its accentuation (such as the word *man* in *policeman*)

en•do•sperm /en′-dō-spərm/ ***n.*** the tissue that envelops the growing embryo of a seed and supplies nutrients

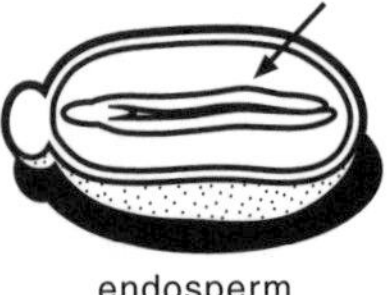

endosperm

end•play /end′-plā/ ***n.*** in the card game of bridge, a strategy that forces your opponent to win a trick (cards that are successfully played)

en•hanced meat /in-han(t)st′ mēt/ ***n.*** any meat product (such as turkey, pork, etc.) injected by a meat producer with a solution of water, salt, and sodium phosphate to enhance juiciness and flavor

erect cle•ma•tis /i-rekt′ kle′-mə-təs/ ***n.*** a species of the European free-standing shrub clematis

erec•tion /i-rek′-shən/ ***n.*** a building, bridge, or other structure that has been erected or built

erec•tone /i-rek′-tōn/ ***n.*** one of a group of chemical compounds extracted from an Asian herb

ero•tic ac•id /i-rä′-tik a′-səd/ ***n.*** a common misspelling of ***orotic acid*** ***<Erotic*** (or, more correctly, orotic) ***acid*** was

once synonymous with B13 but is no longer considered to be a true vitamin.>

evec•tion /i-vek′-shən/ ***n.*** a measurable deviation in the moon's orbit around the Earth

ex•tra hea•vy cream /ek′-strə he′-vē krēm/ ***n.*** cream that has 40 percent or more butterfat

ex•tra jus /ek′-strə jəs/ ***n.*** beyond the law; more than the law requires

ex•tra-vir•gin /ek′-strə-vər′-jən/ ***adj.*** a type of olive oil with an acidity level of 1 percent or less

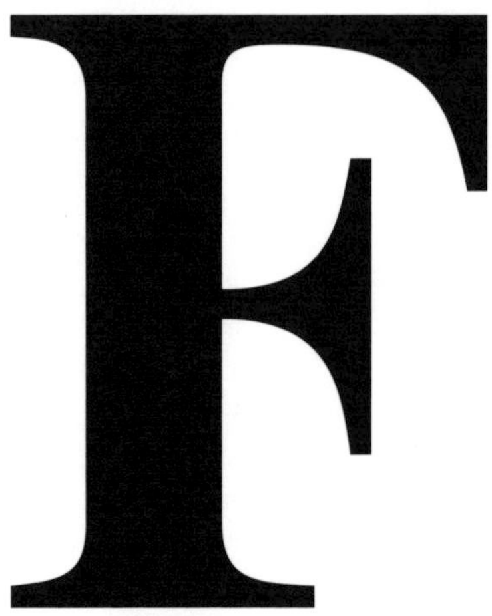

fag end /fag end/ ***n.*** the frayed, coarse, or worn-out end of fabric, as opposed to the finer, sharper end; more broadly, the lesser-quality end of any manufactured product

fan•ny pack /fa′-nē pak/ ***n.*** a purse with its own belt, usually cinched about the waist

Feast of the Ass /fēst əv t͟hē as/ ***n.*** a Catholic holiday, celebrated from the eleventh to the fifteenth centuries every January 14 throughout Europe, to commemorate the infant Christ's escape from King Herod and into the land of Egypt; ***also known as*** Festum Asinorum

fe•male pipe /fē′-māl pīp/ ***n.*** a threaded coupling that joins together two pipes

f-holes /ef′-hōlz/ ***n.*** two f-shaped holes cut into the front of stringed instruments such as violins, viols, cellos, and basses to improve tonal quality; in stringed instruments such as guitars, mandolins, lutes, and so on, sound holes are usually circular, not f-shaped.

firm•ware /fərm′-wer/ ***n.*** read-only-memory (ROM) computer chips that permanently store operating instructions and enable a computer to function properly; different from random-access-memory (RAM) computer chips, which lose stored data as soon as power is shut off

fist jam /fist jam/ ***n.*** a rock-climbing technique in which the climber firmly wedges his or her fist into an available rock crack and then hoists up the entire body using sheer muscle power

flesh plug /flesh pləg/ ***n.*** a flared metal ring used in body piercing that is designed for placement in the lobe, or fatty bottom portion, of the ear

flush•ing hole /flə′-shiŋ hōl/ ***n.*** a hole through an electrode used for introducing dielectric fluid, which conducts electrical force lines but does not conduct electrical current

fly blow /flī blō/ ***n.*** the egg or larva of a blowfly

fook sao /fük saû/ ***n.*** [Chinese phrase meaning "controlling arm"] in the Chinese martial art of kung fu, a term that describes a foxlike movement in which the attacker punches with fingers downward, keeping the elbows close to the ribs for self-protection

force•meat /fôrs′-mēt/ ***n.*** a concoction made of chopped meat, poultry, fish, or produce that is seasoned with herbs and spices, pureed into a creamy paste, and used for stuffing

fore•bulge /fôr′-bəlj/ ***n.*** in geology, an upward land displacement <A ***forebulge*** is created when a massive weight, such as an ice sheet, causes subterranean land to subside or sink deep into the Earth's mantle, between the crust and core, shoving the surface crust upward.>

for•na•cite /fôr′-nə-sīt/ ***n.*** a mineral composed of a basic chromate-arsenate compound

for•ni•cate gy•rus /fôr′-nə-kət jī′-rəs/ ***n.*** a ridge located on the cerebral cortex (brain) of humans and other animals <The ***fornicate gyrus*** gets its name from the fornix, an area of brain matter that loops just underneath the gyrus. Many scientists believe that the fornicate gyrus and other gyri are responsible for controlling the actions of muscles.>

frenched /frencht/ ***adj.*** food cut into long, thin strips

French grip /french grip/ ***n.*** in fencing, a traditional hilt with a slightly curved grip

frui•tar•i•ans /frü-ter′-ē-ənz/ ***n.*** a subgroup of vegans who eat only fruit

fuc•ang•long /fü′-kaŋ-lôŋ/ ***n.*** the legendary mythical Chinese dragons of the underworld

fucanglong

fuch•sin /fyük′-sən/ ***n.*** a magenta dye

fuch•site /fük′-sīt/ ***n.*** a green chromium-rich mineral

fuc•i•tol /fyü′-sə-tôl/ ***n.*** a sugar alcohol made from seaweed

fu•cus /fyü′-kəs/ ***n.*** a type of brown algae

Fu•ka•lite /fü′-kə-līt/ ***n.*** a rare calcium silico-carbonate mineral from Fuka, Japan

fur•be•low /fər′-bə-lō/ ***n.*** another word for a hairball, or a ball of fur in an animal's intestines, created over time by the animal's licking and grooming of its coat

fut•tock /fə′-tək/ ***n.*** a curved piece of wood that helps form the ribs of a ship

fuzz•balls /fəz′-bôlz/ ***n.*** a theoretical astronomical phenomenon similar to the concept of black holes, which are collapsed stars with such an intense gravitational pull that not even light can escape from them

fuzz•box /fəz′-bäks/ ***n.*** an electrical device that changes or distorts the sound of an electric guitar <A ***fuzzbox*** produces rich harmonics or pitches prized by guitarists.>

fuzz but•ton /fəz bə′-tən/ ***n.*** a high-quality electrical contact used in electrical tests

fuzzy front end /fə′-zē frənt end/ ***n.*** in business, a colloquial term used to describe a difficult period of development

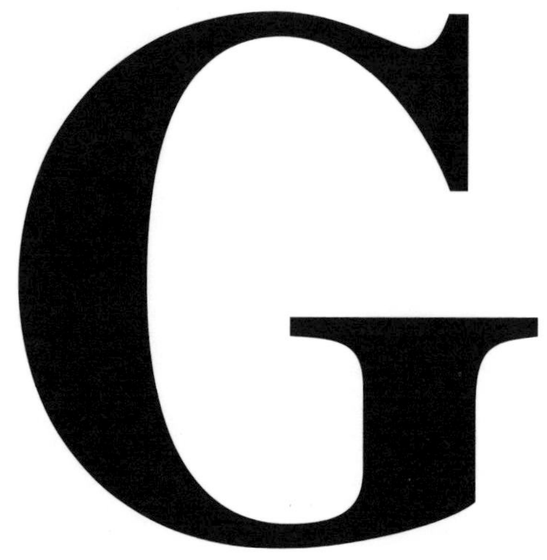

gas cock /gas käk/ ***n.*** a device for turning on and off a flow of natural gas

gas crack•er /gas kra′-kər/ ***n.*** a device that electrically separates the molecules of a liquid into their constituent atoms, usually resulting in a gas <A ***gas cracker*** is used to separate water into hydrogen and oxygen; such gases can then be stored in tanks and sold commercially.>

gen•ti•an•el•la /jen(t)-shə-nel′-ə/ ***n.*** a plant that grows in mountainous regions and is characterized by glossy green leaves and beautiful bell-shaped flowers, which range from lilac to deep blue

girl•cott /gərl′-kät/ ***n.*** a type of boycott by women of a company or an event for political reasons

give him his head /giv him hiz hed/ ***vb.*** to let someone do what he wants

give suck /giv sək/ ***vb.*** to breast-feed a baby

goat•suck•er /gōt′-sə-kər/ ***n.*** any of several large-billed birds of the family Caprimulgidae, including the whippoorwill, that come out at night to feed

go•fu•ku /gō-fü-kü′/ ***n.*** [Japanese word] traditional Japanese clothing

go off half-cocked /gō ôf haf-käkt′/ ***vb. phrase*** to do something reckless or violent without thinking

grease cock /grēs käk/ ***n.*** a machine cock containing grease that serves as a lubricator

great tit /grāt tit/ ***n.*** the largest member of the tit, or Paridae, family of passerine songbirds found throughout Asia and Europe having a black-and-white feathered head and a yellow breast dissected by a black line <The ***great tit*** will build its nest in virtually any available hole, making it a widespread and successful species.>

great tit

grind or•gan /grīnd ôr′-gən/ ***n.*** a mechanical musical instrument that produces sounds by turning a cylinder lined with pegs

ground•nuts /graûnd′-nətz/ ***n.*** an alternative term for peanuts; used chiefly in Great Britain

gym•no•sperm /jim′-nō-spərm/ ***n.*** [From the Greek word *gumnospermos*, meaning "naked seeds"] a member of a group of flowerless seed-bearing plants, the seeds of which appear on the bare edges of cones, such as the Douglas fir pinecone

hairy dar•ling pea /her′-ē där′-liŋ pē/ ***n.*** a rare perennial flowering shrub with pink or purple pea flowers that grows primarily in southern Australia

hairy tongue /her′-ē təŋ/ ***n.*** a growth on the tongue, sometimes caused by antibiotic use

hairy wood•peck•er /her′-ē wûd′-pe-kər/ ***n.*** a type of woodpecker with black and white feathers

hand pump /hand pəmp/ ***n.*** a device used in containers to manually pump thick-viscosity liquids

hand tool /hand tül/ ***n.*** a manually operated, as opposed to power-operated, tool

hard black /härd blak/ ***adj.*** usually written HB on pencils to denote a hard lead

hard•en your ve•hi•cle /här′-dən yər vē′-ə-kəl/ ***vb.*** to make your car more difficult for thieves to burglarize

hard up /härd əp/ ***adj.*** to be very poor or temporarily out of funds

head•butt /hed′-bət/ ***n.*** in boxing, a powerful (albeit illegal) strike with your cranium to an opponent's head

head•mas•ter /hed′-mas-tər/ ***n.*** the male principal or lead teacher of a school

> "To sacrifice a hair of the head of your vision . . . in deference to some Headmaster with a silver pot in his hand . . . is the most abject treachery."
>
> —VIRGINIA WOOLF, *A ROOM OF ONE'S OWN*

head•mis•tress /hed′-mis-trəs/ ***n.*** the female principal or lead teacher of a school

heavy whip•ping cream /he′-vē wi′-piŋ krēm/ ***n.*** a cream with a measured butterfat content of approximately 36–40 percent <Supermarkets today generally carry only light whipping cream, with a lower butterfat content, but ***heavy whipping cream*** is often available upon request.>

het•ero•ga•met•ic sex /he-tə-rō-gə-me′-tik seks/ ***n.*** the male gender, which has two different chromosomes

high stick•ing /hī sti′-kiŋ/ ***vb.*** in the game of hockey, to carry your stick well above regulation height

hoar /hôr/ ***n.*** a coating of frosty white ice crystals on any surface; ***also***, gray, or having gray, hair

hoary /hôr′-ē/ ***adj.*** white, gray, or grayish white; old

hoe /hō/ ***n.*** a tool with a sharp flat blade for digging in the earth

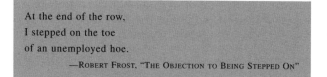

> At the end of the row,
> I stepped on the toe
> of an unemployed hoe.
>
> —Robert Frost, "The Objection to Being Stepped On"

hoe•cake /hō′-kāk/ ***n.*** cornbread originally baked on the blade of a hoe by enslaved Africans during the Civil War, and possibly much earlier <Southern slaves sympathetic to invading Union troops often served fresh-baked ***hoecakes*** to the hungry soldiers.>

hoe•down /hō′-daûn/ ***n.*** a happy, energetic dance

hole punch /hōl pənch/ ***n.*** a device for punching holes in multiple sheets of paper

ho•me•o•mor•phism /hō-mē-ə-môr′-fi-zəm/ ***n.*** in topology, the similar or identical nature of different structures

ho•mo /hō′-mō/ ***n.*** in biology, the genus that includes modern humans

Homo erectus

Ho•mo erec•tus /hō′-mō i-rek′-təs/ ***n.*** an evolutionary ancestor of homo sapiens, or modern humans

ho•mog•amy /hō-mä′-gə-mē/ ***n.*** a union or marriage between two individuals who share a similar culture

ho•mo•graph /hä′-mə-graf/ ***n.*** a word spelled like another word but different in meaning or pronunciation (as in, a *sow* /sou/ is a female pig, but to *sow* /sō/ seeds)

ho•mol•o•gate /hō-mä′-lə-gāt/ ***vb.*** to offer approval, to sanction

ho•mol•o•graph•ic /hō-mä-lə-graf′-ik/ ***adj.*** a type of projection in which all components of a map or diagram are accurately depicted in terms of their relative shapes and sizes

ho•mol•o•gy /hō-mä′-lə-jē/ ***n.*** a similarity or correlation between differing systems, particularly systems of human belief

ho•mo•phone /hä′-mə-fōn/ ***n.*** a word pronounced like another word but different in spelling and meaning (as in *sun* and *son*)

hon•eypot /hə′-nē-pät/ ***n.*** a beeswax container made by a queen bumblebee to store honey. <The queen bee feeds from the ***honeypot*** while caring for her eggs.>

hore•hound /hôr′-haûnd/ ***n.*** an aromatic Eurasian plant of the mint family

Hor Fun /hôr fün/ ***n.*** a thick broad Chinese rice noodle, originally created in Shahe, China, which is now part of Guangzhou, China; ***also known as*** *shahe fen and ho fun* <***Hor Fun*** noodles are generally stir-fried in hot oil and added to eggs, shrimp, and vegetables to produce the world-famous entrée pad thai.>

hor•nist /hôr′-nist/ ***n.*** a musician who plays a brass horn, particularly the French horn

hor•ny frog /hôr′-nē frôg/ ***n.*** in zoology, any of several types of insectivorous (insect-eating) lizards found in the remote deserts of the United States

hor•ny goat weed /hôr′-nē gōt wēd/ ***n.*** a type of herbaceous plant of the genus *Epimedium*

hor•ny-hand•ed /hôr-nē-han′-dəd/ ***adj.*** the condition of a person whose hands are calloused from hard physical labor

hor•ny layer /hôr′-nē lā′-ər/ ***n.*** the outermost layer of the epidermis (skin)

hot rod /hät räd/ ***n.*** a homebuilt performance-enhanced car, usually an older model

hot sauce /hät sôs/ ***n.*** a chili-pepper-based sauce used for making foods spicier

hug•ger-mug•ger•ing /hə-gər-mə′-gər-iŋ/ ***vb.*** to act in a secretive manner

hum•bug•gery /həm-bə′-gə-rē/ ***n.*** the act of imposing on someone or something; ***also***, to defraud someone

ice screw /īs skrü/ ***n.*** a large, specially designed metal screw used by mountain climbers while ascending or descending to help anchor ropes to icy cliffs

im•preg•na•ble /im-preg′-nə-bəl/ ***adj.*** unable to be forcefully entered or broken into, as a fortress or prison

in•ser•tion /in-sər-shən/ ***n.*** in arts and crafts, an item of lace sewn onto a larger piece of cloth for ornamentation

in•ter•bas•ta•tion /in′-tər-bas-tā′-shən/ ***n.*** a patchwork quilt

in•vag•i•nate /in-va′-jə-nāt/ ***vb.*** [From the Latin word *vagina*, meaning "sheath" or "scabbard"] to put something into something else, typically a sword into a scabbard

jack•fruit /jak′-früt/ ***n.*** an east Indian tree of the mulberry family

jack•screw /jak′-skrü/ ***n.*** a hand-cranked or hydraulic device used to raise objects several feet or yards into the air; ***also called*** screw jack <The threaded rod of a ***jackscrew*** turns through a nut held by movable metal bars connected to a metal plate. This arrangement effectively raises extremely heavy loads such as cars and trucks.>

Ja•cob's rod /jā′-kəbz räd/ ***n.*** any of a genus of plants of the lily family; the asphodel

jac•ti•ta•tion /jak-ti-tā′-shən/ ***n.*** boasting falsely; ***also***, spasmodic movements due to a discomfiting illness

jam nut /jam nət/ ***n.*** a nut that provides extra resistance to vibration from machinery

jaw•bon•ing /jô′-bō-ning/ ***n.*** an official using the prestige of office to influence others, as in a mayor suggesting a new public-schools policy

Je•ru•sa•lem cher•ry /jə-rü′-sə-ləm cher′-ē/ ***n.*** the *Solanum pseudocapsicum* plant, which produces poisonous red fruit resembling tomatoes

jock•ey pump /jä′-kē pəmp/ ***n.*** a small pump connected to a sprinkler system

joy stick /joi stik/ ***n.*** the upright lever that controls an aircraft or a computer video game

jug•han•dle /jəg han′-d^{ə}l/ ***n.*** a roadway where cars make left turns utilizing a right-lane exit just before an intersection—the exit loops around like a jug handle, allowing cars to travel through the intersection and across the original road

jug hold /jəg hôld/ ***n.*** in rock climbing, a large, easily grasped handhold on a rock face

jug hold

jug•u•late /jü′-gyə-lāt/ ***vb.*** in medicine, to use heroic or desperate measures to defeat a stubborn illness

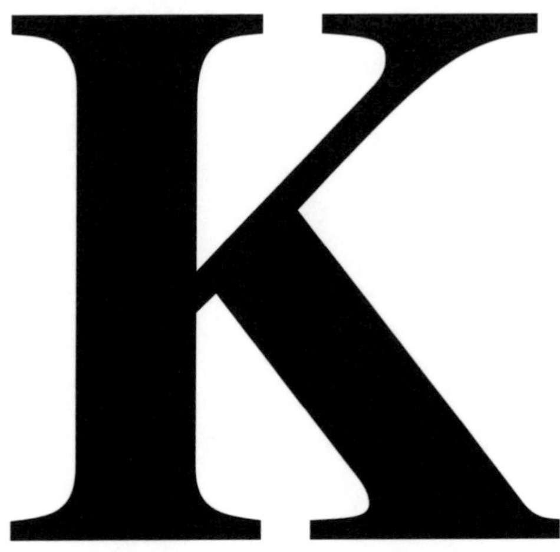

kick•ball (kik′-bôl) ***n.*** a game played by kicking a rubber ball and running to bases

kinky /kiŋ′-kē/ ***adj.*** curly textured hair; ***also***, anything wiry or curly

kiss•ing the gun•ner's daugh•ter /ki′-siŋ <u>th</u>ə gə′-nərz dô′-tər/ ***vb.*** to bend over a cannon's barrel for punitive caning or flogging

Kum•mer the•o•ry (kəm′-ər thir′-ï) ***n.*** a set of beliefs that incorporates the general theory of quadratic extensions <The ***Kummer theory*** was originally developed in the 1840s by the German mathematician Ernst Kummer.>

kum•quat /kəm′-kwät/ ***n.*** a tiny fruit of the flowering kumquat tree, a member of the genus *Fortunella*, related to the genus *Citrus*; ***also*** cumquat <A ***kumquat*** looks like a miniature orange but is more oval and may vary in color from green to red. Because of its sweet-tasting rind and flesh, the kumquat is often used to make liqueurs and marmalades.>

kunz•ite /kûn(t)′-zīt/ ***n.*** a pinkish lilac crystalline gemstone discovered in 1902 by the American mineralogist George Frederick Kunz (1856–1932) <***Kunzite*** is classified as a type of spodumene, a mineral containing lithium, which is a chemical element compounded to create mood-stabilizing drugs and other commercial products.>

kunzite

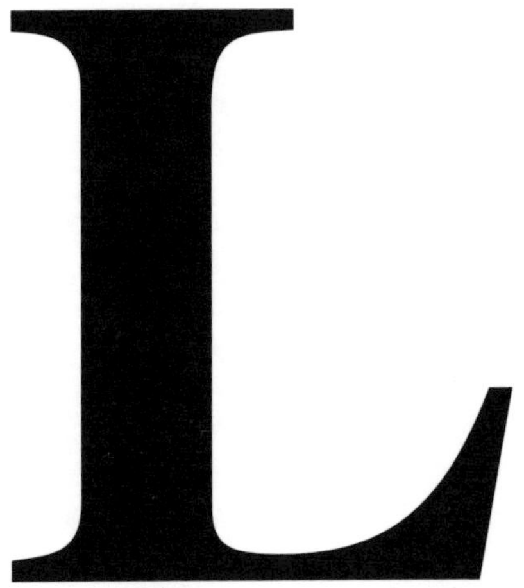

la•bi•al fur•rows /lā′-bē-əl fər′-ōz/ ***n.*** [From the Latin word *labium*, meaning "lips"] in ichthyology (the study of fish), the shallow grooves around the upper and lower lips of fish that create the protruding mouth characteristic of most fish species

la•bi•al•ize /lā′-bē-ə-līz/ ***vb.*** to verbalize consonant and vowel sounds by using one's lips

la•dy's bed•straw /lā′-dēz bed′-strô/ ***n.*** a herbaceous annual plant (*Galium vernum)* characterized by clusters of yellow blooms; once used to stuff mattresses because of the plant's flea-killing properties

lag screw /lag skrü/ ***n.*** a large metal screw with a bolt-like hexagon-shaped head to facilitate ease of turning; ***also called*** lag bolt

lap dog /lap dôg/ ***n.*** a dog sufficiently small that it can be placed comfortably in one's lap

laugh•ing jack•ass /la′-fiŋ jak′-as/ ***n.*** a large bird of the family Halcyonidae that has brown and blue feathers; ***also known as*** kookaburra (*Dacelo novaeguineae*) <The ***laughing jackass*** is found throughout Papua New Guinea and Australia and is famed for its notorious cry, "Ooh-ooh-AH-AH-AH!" The sound strongly resembles laughter and has been included in nearly every exotic adventure movie ever made.>

lay broth•er /lā brə′-thər/ ***n.*** a monk who has taken religious vows but is not yet a full-fledged member of the religious group he aspires to join

lay day /lā dā/ ***n.*** a day allowed for unloading a ship without the assessment of additional fees

lay•wom•an /lā-wû′-mən/ ***n.*** [From the Greek word *laikos*, meaning "of the people"] a woman who studies and trains to become a Catholic nun—that is, a woman who will live in a religious community and devote her life to God, not to a husband or children <A ***laywoman*** is a member of the laity, women who have not yet sworn religious vows and are therefore not yet full-fledged Catholic nuns.>

leg warm•er /leg wôr′-mər/ ***n.*** a knitted covering designed to keep the leg warm

lei /lā/ ***n.*** a Hawaiian garland of flowers usually worn around the neck

les•bi•an ma•son•ry /lez′-bē-ən mā′-sən-rē/ ***n.*** a unique type of masonry construction featuring polygonal stone blocks dressed with curving joints <***Lesbian masonry*** originated on the Greek island of Lesbos, in the Aegean Sea, and dates back to the seventh century BC.>

lic•tor /lik′-tər/ ***n.*** a civil servant in ancient Rome

light whip•ping cream /līt wi′-piŋ krēm/ ***n.*** cream that has enough butterfat (30–36 percent) to be whipped

lip ser•vice /lip sər′-vəs/ ***n.*** a fraudulent pronouncement of solidarity or admiration

lip trick /lip trik/ ***n.*** in skateboarding, a trick done near the lip (edge) of a half-pipe wall

liq•uid pen•e•trant /li′-kwəd pe′-nə-trənt/ ***n.*** a nondestructive testing agent used on nonferrous alloys

load dis•place•ment /lōd dis-plā′-smənt/ ***n.*** the amount of water that a fully loaded cargo ship displaces

lob•cock /läb′-käk/ ***n.*** an eighteenth-century British slang term for a dull, idle person

lock•nut /läk′-nət/ ***n.*** a special nut that is tightened on top of an ordinary nut for additional strength

log•cock /lôg′-käk/ ***n.*** the pileated woodpecker

logcock

log•ger•head /lô′-gər-hed/ ***n.*** a metal pole with a ball on one end; the ball is heated, then used to turn solid pitch into a malleable liquid

loose ball /lüs bôl/ ***n.*** in American football or basketball, a ball that is still in play but has escaped an individual player's possession <A ***loose ball*** generally sends players on both teams scrambling to grab it because it can no longer be played if it goes out of bounds (travels beyond the edges of the football field or the basketball court).>

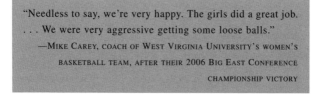

> "Needless to say, we're very happy. The girls did a great job. . . . We were very aggressive getting some loose balls."
>
> —Mike Carey, coach of West Virginia University's women's basketball team, after their 2006 Big East Conference championship victory

loose smut /lüs smət/ ***n.*** in botany, a group of diseases affecting cereal grasses such as corn, oats, rice, and wheat, caused by *Ustilago*, a genus of smut fungi

lo•tus po•si•tion /lō′-təs pə-zi′-shən/ ***n.*** in yoga, a cross-legged sitting position, with the back straight, both legs folded into an X, the feet resting against the thighs, and the fingers lightly touching each knee

love game /ləv gām/ ***n.*** a tennis game in which the loser's score is zero

love knot /ləv nät/ ***n.*** a knot that is difficult to undo

low•ball /lō′-bôl/ ***vb.*** to offer an extremely low price for something in the hopes of getting a bargain

low blow /lō blō/ ***n.*** in boxing, an illegal hit below the belt, or waistline

low•er the boom /lō′-ər t͟hə büm/ ***vb.*** to act forcefully to reprimand someone

lu•cu•brate /lü′-kyə-brāt/ ***vb.*** to study or labor intensively, often long after dark

lun•cheon meat /lən′-chən mēt/ ***n.*** factory-processed meat, such as bologna or salami, that can be used to make sandwiches or other quick meals

mac•er•ate /ma′-sə-rāt/ ***vb.*** in physiology, to digest food in the stomach, saturating it with powerful acids

mag•na cum laude /mäg′-nə kûm laû′-də/ ***adj.*** ranked at the top of a graduating class

Maid•en•head lo•ca•tor sys•tem /mā′-dən-hed lō′-kā-tər sis′-təm/ ***n.*** a system used by radio operators to locate sites on Earth

man cov•er•age /man kəv′-rij/ ***n.*** a football defense in which every player covers, or guards, a specific player on the opposing team

man•han•dle /man′-han-d^{ə}l/ ***vb.*** to transport or shift heavy objects by human muscle-power alone

man•hole /man′-hōl/ ***n.*** a round opening above a cylindrical tunnel through which sewer maintenance workers enter and descend by means of a ladder to make repairs

mas•ti•cate /mas′-tə-kāt/ ***vb.*** to chew, as with food

mas•tiff /mas′-stəf/ ***n.*** a breed of large dogs noted for courage and strength

meat job•ber /mēt jä′-bər/ ***n.*** a restaurant distributor who sells meat supplies

meat•man /mēt′-man/ ***n.*** a seller of various cuts of meat; a butcher

meat pie /mēt pī/ ***n.*** meat, vegetables, and gravy contained in a baked pie crust

mel•on ball•er /me′-lən bô′-lər/ ***n.*** a handheld kitchen tool, usually made of stainless steel, used to scoop out the fruit of melons into little spheres or hemispheres for salads and desserts

me•nag•er•ie /mə-naj′-ə-rē/ ***n.*** an assortment of exotic animals held in captivity and displayed

me•nin•go•coc•cus /mə-niŋ-gə-kä′-kəs/ ***n.*** the bacterium that causes the disease meningitis, a brain infection

men•su•ra•tion /men(t)-sə-rāy′-shən/ ***n.*** [From the Latin *mensurare*, meaning "to measure"] the act of measuring the length, width, angles, area, and volume of geometric shapes; also refers generally to the act of measuring anything

me•so•pause /me′-zə-pôz/ ***n.*** in meteorology, a transitional area in Earth's upper atmosphere <The ***mesopause*** is located about twenty-five miles above the Earth's surface, between the mesosphere (zone of heavy wind activity) and the thermosphere (zone of solar heat absorption).>

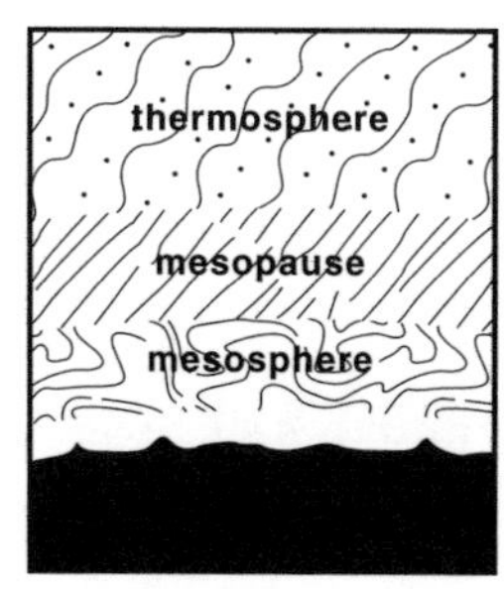

mess•mate /mes′-māt/ ***n.*** a regular dining companion, in any branch of the military service

mi•cro•coc•cus /mī-krō-kä′-kəs/ ***n.*** ovoid bacteria that group together to consume organic tissue

milk leg /milk′ leg/ ***n.*** an agonizing enlargement of the leg muscles generally caused by an infection contracted while giving birth

mon•key nuts /məŋ′-kē nətz/ ***n.*** a British slang term for raw peanuts in their shells

mono•coque /mä′-nə-käk/ ***adj.*** the metal covering of a rocket or aircraft that bears the stresses the craft is subject to as it navigates the Earth's atmosphere or outer space

moor•cock /mûr′-käk/ ***n.*** a male of the red grouse or moorfowl group of birds; ***also called*** ptarmigan

mor•ass /mə-ras′/ ***n.*** a swampy wetland; ***also***, a confusing situation that is difficult to extricate oneself from

moth•er lode /mə′-thər lōd/ ***n.*** a principal vein from which gold ore is mined

moth•er tongue /mə′-t͟hər təŋ/ ***n.*** one's first spoken language learned in childhood

mouse ball /maûs bôl/ ***n.*** a hard rubber ball that rolls inside a computer's mouse (pointing device)

mouth or•gan /maûth ôr′-gən/ ***n.*** a harmonica, or small rectangular wind instrument played with the mouth

muff /məf/ ***n.*** a warm tube-shaped covering for the hands that is usually made of fur

mul•ti•vi•bra•tor /məl-tē-vī′-brā-tər/ ***n.*** a particular type of electrical circuit that contains a pair of transistors, or devices that control the flow of electricity

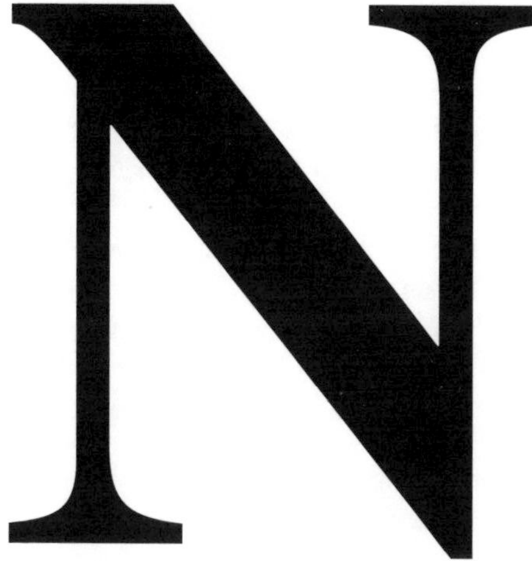

na•ked buck•wheat /nā′-kəd bək′-wēt/ ***n.*** a shrub of the wild buckwheat genus

na•ked con•fes•sion /nā′-kəd kən-fe′-shən/ ***n.*** an occurrence in which a person confesses to a crime, but no evidence supports the confession

na•ked•head /nā′-kəd-hed/ ***n.*** a type of osmeriforme (ray-finned) fish of the family Alepocephalidae that lives in the Atlantic, Pacific, and Indian oceans; ***also called*** slickhead <The fish is called a ***nakedhead*** because it lacks the hard scales found on the heads of many other fish species. Extensively studied members of the family include Baird's smooth-head (*Alepocephalus bairdii*) and the softskin smooth-head (*Rouleina attrita*)>

na•ked mole rat /nā′-kəd mōl rat/ ***n.*** a hairless burrowing rodent common in east Africa

na•ked short•ing /nā′-kəd shôrt′-iŋ/ ***n.*** a financial term for a controversial method of selling securities; also known as naked short selling <Selling short occurs when a seller contracts to sell securities he or she doesn't own but has paid to "borrow." The short seller hopes the price of the securities will go down, not up, so that he may buy them back at the reduced price and pocket the difference. For example, suppose shares of Company A sell for $10 apiece. A short seller pays cash to borrow 100 Company A shares, then quickly sells them to someone else for $1000. If the shares go down to $5 apiece, the short seller buys back 100 shares for $500, returns the shares to the first owner, and makes $500 in profit. But in ***naked shorting***, the seller not only doesn't own the securities but hasn't even paid to borrow them. That makes naked shorting controversial, with some critics charging fraud, while others claim the practice weeds out overvalued stocks.>

nas•tic move•ment /nas′-tik müv′-mənt/ ***n.*** in botany, a plant movement that is not in the direction of a stimulus, such as sunlight, but away from it

nat•u•ral gas /na′-chə-rəl gas/ ***n.*** a combination of methane and other hydrocarbons that is burned for cooking, heating, and transportation

night•stick /nīt′-stik/ ***n.*** the baton used by a police officer to subdue criminal suspects

nipplefruit

nip•ple•fruit /ni′-pəl-früt/ ***n.*** a plant of the family Solanaceae found throughout South America and the Caribbean <The ***nipplefruit*** is genetically related to tomatoes but is poisonous and inedible. The plant features large bulbous fruit, culminating in slender delicate tips.>

nip•ple gong /ni′-pəl gäŋ/ ***n.*** a small metal gong with a raised boss, or nipple, in the center

nose•gay /nōz′-gā/ ***n.*** a small bouquet of fragrant flowers given as a gift; ***also known as*** tussie-mussie or posey <Originally, in the Middle Ages, Europeans wore ***nosegays*** on their lapels to hide the reeking odors of raw sewage, horse manure, etc., that were abundant at the time.>

> "I have here only made a nosegay of culled flowers and have brought nothing of my own but the thread that ties them together."
>
> —MICHEL EYQUEM DE MONTAIGNE, ***ESSAYS***

nu•di•branch /nü-də-braŋk′/ ***n.*** [from the Latin word *nudus*, meaning "nude," and the ancient Greek word *brankhia*, meaning "gills"] a sea slug featuring sensitive tentacles on its head and a brightly colored, undulating body <The word ***nudibranch*** relates to the slug's act of breathing through fleshy plumes on its backs, not through gills.>

nut•crack•er /nət′-kra-kər/ ***n.*** a device for cracking open nut shells

nut di•la•tion /nət dī-lā′-shən/ ***n.*** the widening or expansion of a nut as it wedges tightly against a bolt

nut hand /nət hand/ ***n.*** in the card game of poker, the strongest hand at any one time

nut•hatch /nət′-hach/ ***n.*** one of the birds of the family Sittidae characterized by small tails and sharp bills

nut•meat /nət′-mēt/ ***n.*** the edible flesh found in the center of any nut

nut•pick /nət′-pik/ ***n.*** a slender metal instrument with a sharp tip or point for digging out a nut's nutritious kernel after the nut's hard outer shell has been cracked

nut rais•er /nət rā′-zər/ ***n.*** a guitarist's device for elevating guitar strings above a fret board

nut run•ner /nət rə′-nər/ ***n.*** an air-compressed, torque-controlled tool for tightening fasteners

nut•ting /nət′-iŋ/ ***vb.*** to gather nuts

nyc•tin•as•ty /nik′-tə-nas-tē/ ***n.*** in botany, the rapid opening and closing of flower-petals, sometimes observable within minutes <***Nyctinasty*** is caused by the rising and setting of the sun, or by other variations in light, producing chemical changes and a resultant physical movement. Nyctinastic plants close their petals at night and open them in daytime. Common nyctinastic plants are mimosa (*Mimosa pudica*) and clover (*Trifolium repens*).>

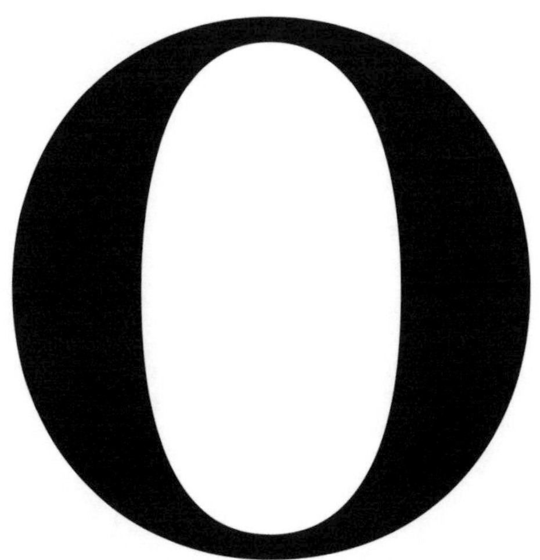

Oil Thigh /oil thī/ ***n.*** the unofficial title of the famous chorale "Queen's College Colours" sung by the students of Queen's University in Kingston, Ontario, Canada, during sporting events; the song's colloquial title derives from the Gaelic refrain *Oil thigh na Banrighinn a'Banrighinn gu brath* ("The college of the queen forever")

o•o•sperm /ō′-ə-spərm/ ***n.*** an alternative name for a zygote, or a fertilized human embryo

o•pen•hole /ō′-pən-hōl/ ***n.*** in oil-well drilling, the uncased part of an oil well, or the part that has not yet been reinforced with heavy metal pipe

o•pen•hole pack•er /ō′-pən-hōl pa′-kər/ ***n.*** in oil-well drilling, a specific type of packer, or a device that is inserted into a borehole and that then expands to seal the hole

o•pen po•si•tion /ō′-pən pə-zi′-shən/ ***n.*** in dancing, any position in which the couple stands apart

open position

or•gan grind•er /ôr′-gən grīn′-dər/ ***n.*** a street musician who plays a cylindrical instrument called a barrel organ

or•gan•i•cism /ôr-ga′-nə-si-zəm/ ***n.*** a biological doctrine that says life results from the whole physiological system of an organism, not from its separate, individual organs

or•gan•ism /ôr′-gə-ni-zəm/ ***n.*** an individual, composed of various organ systems

or•gan meat /ôr′-gən mēt/ ***n.*** the internal organs of butchered livestock, excluding muscles; ***also known as*** offal <***Organ meat*** may be either discarded or sold as a rare delicacy, depending on the local market.>

or•gan•za /ôr-gan′-zə/ ***n.*** a sheer dress fabric, usually made of silk

out•gass•ing /aût′-ga-siŋ/ ***vb.*** to release gases from a planet's interior into its atmosphere

ox•peck•er /äks′-pe-kər/ ***n.*** a type of African bird of the subfamily Buphaginae

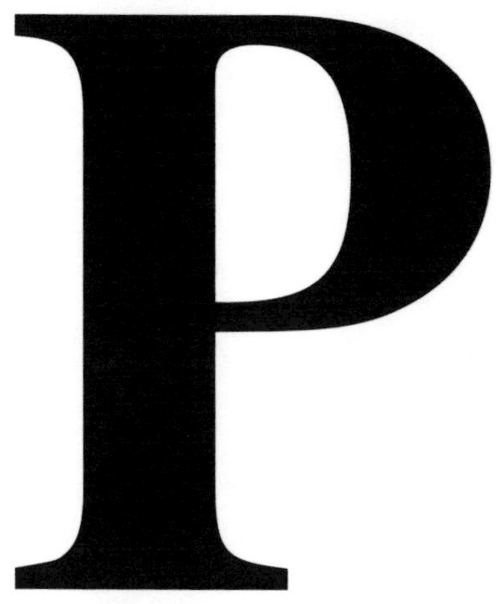

pal•i•asse /pal′-yas/ ***n.*** a crude mattress stuffed with sawdust

pan•sper•mia /pan-spər′-mē-ə/ ***n.*** the theory that the elementary "seeds of life" disseminate throughout all intergalactic space

pan•sy /pan′-zē/ ***n.*** a type of violet cultivated from the wildflower heartsease (*Viola tricolor*) as a hybrid for display in gardens <A ***pansy*** has five large delicate petals, and different hybrids range from white to yellow with reddish centers, as well as deep blue with purple centers.>

part•ner•ing /pärt′-nər-iŋ/ ***vb.*** to lift or carry a partner, as when a male ballet dancer lifts a ballerina

par•ty poop•er /pär′-tē pü′-pər/ ***n.*** someone too tired or lethargic to participate in a festive gathering

pea /pē/ ***n.*** a tiny, spherical, green vegetable

pea•cock /pē′-käk/ ***n.*** the male of the peafowl bird species, noted for its beautiful tail feathers

pea•shoot•er /pē′-shü-tər/ ***n.*** a child's toy made from a tubular straw and used to blow peas or other small projectiles at high velocity

ped•a•go•gy /pe-də-gō′-jē/ ***n.*** the art of educating children in reading, writing, mathematics, and other academic disciplines

ped•o•don•tist /pe-də-dän′-tist/ ***n.*** a dentist who specializes in treating children's teeth

peep sight /pēp sīt/ ***n.*** a gun-sight placed on the back of a rifle or handgun that uses a small circle aligned with another gun-sight in front

pee•wit /pē′-wit/ ***n.*** a small bird named for its distinctive cry; ***also called*** lapwing

pe•nal /pē′-nəl/ ***adj.*** having to do with penalties or prison

pe•nal la•bor /pē′-nəl lā′-bər/ ***n.*** hard labor used as a form of punishment for convicted criminals

pe•nal ser•vi•tude /pē′-nəl sər′-və-tüd/ ***n.*** a jail term featuring the imposition of hard physical labor as punishment

pen•e•trance /pe′-nə-trən(t)s/ ***n.*** in genetics, a measurement of how frequently a particular gene affects the organisms that carry the gene

pen•e•tra•tion depth /pe-nə-trā′-shun depth/ ***n.*** the depth that electromagnetic radiation penetrates into a material

pe•nol•o•gy /pē-näl′-ə-jē/ ***n.*** the study of prison administration and the rehabilitation of prisoners

pe•on /pē′-än/ ***n.*** a virtual slave forced into bondage to satisfy unpaid debts

pet•cock /pet′-käk/ ***n.*** a valve that releases pressure from a steam boiler

pe•tro•phile /pe′-trə-fīl/ ***n.*** an oil-consuming microorganism used in the cleanup of oil spills <According to recent scientific testing, the most effective ***petrophile*** appears to be the *Pseudomonas* bacteria.>

phag•o•cyte /fa′-gə-sīt/ ***n.*** [From the Greek word *phagein*, meaning "to eat"] in cytology (the study of microscopic cells), a colorless blood cell that attacks and eats foreign material in blood, whether invasive germs or other harmful detritus <The ***phagocyte*** is essential to the human immune system, which is the set of biological defenses that fight infection and disease.>

phag•o•cy•to•sis /fa-gə-sī-tō′-səs/ ***n.*** the phenomenon that occurs when phagocyte cells surround and eat invading organisms

phal•lus im•pu•dic•us /fa′-ləs im-pyü′-də-kəs/ ***n.*** a type of fungus that produces rod-shaped mushrooms

pho•nog•ra•phy /fə-nä′-grə-fē/ ***n.*** written representations of the sounds of speech

phoque /fôk/ ***n.*** [French word] a fur-covered aquatic mammal; a seal

phoque

pi•an•ism /pē′-ə-ni-zəm/ ***n.*** a piano player's musical artistry

pi•an•ist /pē-a′-nist/ ***n.*** one who plays the piano

pig•eon pea /pi′-jən pē/ ***n.*** the *Cajanus cajan* plant, related to the pea plant; found primarily in the tropics

pinch•cock /pinch′-käk/ ***n.*** a valve on a flexible tube used to regulate the flow of fluids

pink ball /piŋk bôl/ ***n.*** in the billiard game of snooker, the pink ball worth six points

pink cock•a•too /piŋk kä′-kə-tü/ ***n.*** an Australian cockatoo with pink-tinged feathers

pink fai•ry arm•a•dil•lo /piŋk fer′-ē är-mə-di′-lō/ ***n.*** a type of armadillo, a mammal of the species *Dasypodidae*

pink-head•ed duck /piŋk-he′-dəd dək/ ***n.*** a large diving duck native to India

pink of my John /piŋk əv mī jän/ ***n.*** a common European herb from which most pansy hybrids are derived

pink sheets /piŋk shēts/ ***n.*** a publication listing the prices of over-the-counter shares of stock

pip /pip/ ***n.*** any tiny seed, such as that from an apple

piss•as•phalt /pis′-as-fôlt/ ***n.*** a soft black bitumen with the consistency of tar

poop deck /püp dek/ ***n.*** the elevated deck at the rear, or stern, of a sailing ship

pooped /püpt/ ***adj.*** weary, out of energy

prick post /prik pōst/ ***n.*** an archaic architectural term for a queen post, one of the two upright support posts in a queen-post roof truss; the two upper ends are usually bound together by a cable or rod

prick song /prik sôŋ/ ***n.*** a musical composition written with dots or points rather than standard musical notation

> "Oh hee's the Couragious Captain of Complements: he fights as you sing prick song."
>
> —William Shakespeare, *Romeo and Juliet*

P

Pri•vate Bag /prī′-vət bag/ ***n.*** an alternative term for a ***Private Mail Bag***, a type of high-volume postal delivery service common in many countries (particularly Australia, New Zealand, and South Africa) and generally used by large organizations such as corporations or governments

pro•phy•lax•is /prō-fə-lak′-səs/ ***n.*** [From the Greek word *prophylaktikos*, meaning "to guard or prevent"] a medical regimen to forestall disease rather than treat it after the fact; for example, applying an antibiotic cream to a burn to prevent potential infections

Pschitt /p(ə)shit′/ ***n.*** a brand of French soda pop

puck /pək/ ***n.*** a hard rubber disk that hockey players try to shoot through a goal

puck•er /pə′-kər/ ***vb.*** to form the lips into a small circle, usually before a kiss

puck•fist /pək′-fist/ ***n.*** a type of sphere-shaped fungus that contains dustlike spores

puckfist

pulled pork /pûld pôrk/ ***n.*** pork shoulder meat cooked until it is tender enough to be shredded with a fork; usually served with barbecue sauce

pump and dump /pəmp ənd dəmp/ ***vb.*** to fraudulently advertise inflated stock prices, then sell the stock with the intent to make a profit

pump or•gan /pəmp ôr′-gən/ ***n.*** a musical keyboard-organ with air supplied by a foot pump

pu•pa /pyü′-pə/ ***n.*** the dormant form of an insect

pu•pu plat•ter /pü′-pü pla′-tər/ ***n.*** [From the Hawaiian word *pupu*, meaning "appetizers"] a round wooden platter of Hawaiian hors d'oeuvres or appetizers that has a pink or blue flame issuing from a central bowl <The ***pupu platter*** is served before a meal's main course and may contain tidbits of pork, vegetables, fruit, etc.>

Pu•sey•ism /pyü′-zē-i-zəm/ ***n.*** the collected teachings and beliefs of Dr. Edward Bouverie Pusey, one of the most influential preachers of the Church of England (Anglican Church) <From his post at Oriel College, part of the University of Oxford in Great Britain, Dr. Pusey preached sermons and authored treatises collectively labeled ***Puseyism*** by his devoted followers. As part of the broader Oxford Movement embraced by like-minded theologians, Puseyism taught that Anglicans should return to venerable theological concepts and reject rationalism—the notion that human reason may be employed in lieu of reliance on scripture.>

pus•sy•toes /pû′-sē-tōz/ ***n.*** an alternative name for the genus *Antennaria* of herbaceous perennial plants

pus•sy wil•low /pû′-sē wi′-lō/ ***n.*** either of two types of willow trees bearing velvety flowers: the *Salix discolor* found throughout North America or the *Salix caprea* found throughout Europe

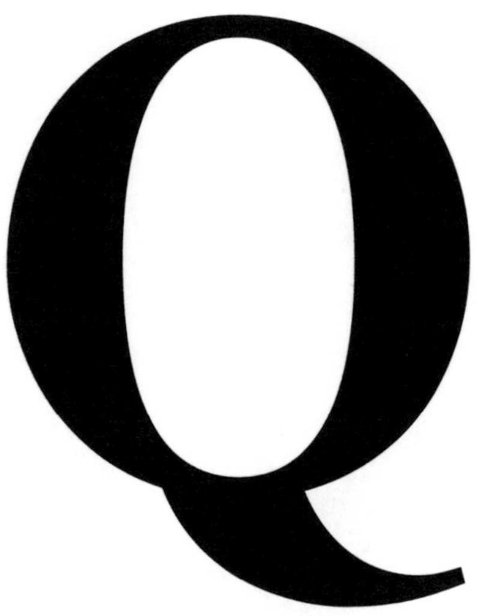

quae•re /kwir′-ē/ ***n.*** alternate spelling of ***query***, a question

queen•ing /kwē′-niŋ/ ***vb.*** the act of a cat giving birth

queer for /kwir fôr/ ***adj.*** to really want something very much; to be obsessed

quick load /kwik lōd/ ***n.*** a video-game feature that enables a player to load a saved game by pressing a button that immediately continues the saved game

quin•cunx /kwin′-kuŋ(k)s/ ***n.*** a game with a glass face, metal pins, and rolling balls; similar to the Asian game of *pachinko*

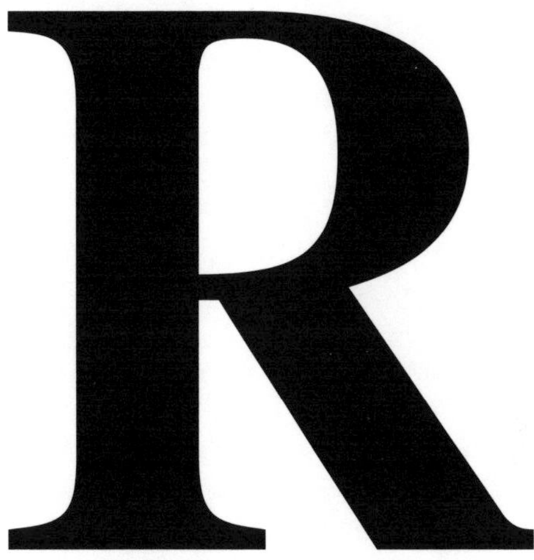

ram•i•fi•ca•tion /ra-mə-fə-kā′-shən/ ***n.*** a possible meaning and consequence of a course of action

ram•rod /ram′-räd/ ***n.*** a rod used to compact the explosive powder in muzzle-loaded guns

range balls /rānj bôlz/ ***n.*** golf balls used for practice purposes only

rear-end /rir-end′/ ***vb.*** to hit the back of someone's car with a vehicle

rear horse /rir hôrs/ ***n.*** an alternative name for the insect called the praying mantis

rec•ti•fy /rek′-tə-fī/ ***vb.*** to make things right

red-breast•ed nut•hatch /red′-bres-təd nət′-hach/ ***n.*** a bluish gray bird with a red breast

re•nal /rē′-nəl/ ***adj.*** of or pertaining to the kidneys, the two C-shaped internal organs that separate wastes from the bloodstream and flush them out of the body as urine

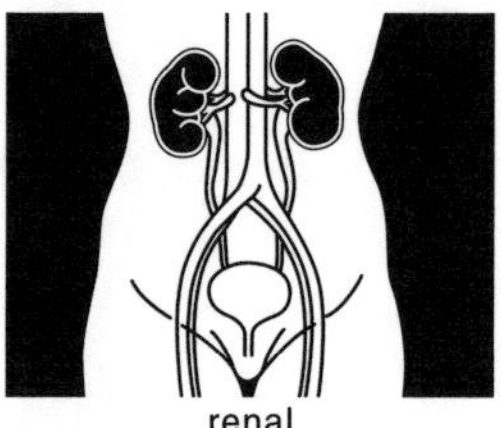
renal

ridge•pole /rij′-pōl/ ***n.*** the term for the long piece of wood that forms a gabled roof's ridgeline, or apex

ris•er /rī′-zər/ ***n.*** the upright portion of a step

ro•bus•ta beans /rō-bəs′-tə bēnz/ ***n.*** the supermarket-grade coffee beans grown in tropical climates

roc•ball /rôk′-bôl/ ***n.*** a modern ball game modeled after the centuries-old ball games of the Aztec Indians

rods /rädz/ ***n.*** in anatomy, the light receptors in the eyes of primates

ru•basse /rü′-bas/ ***n.*** a type of quartz with red iron oxide

rub•bage /rə′-bij/ ***n.*** an alternative spelling of ***rubbish***; trash, garbage

rub•bing in /rə′-biŋ in/ ***vb.*** in cooking, the incorporation of fat into flour

ru•bri•cate /rü′-bri-kāt/ ***vb.*** [From the Latin word *rubrico*, meaning "to color red"] to use red ink to inscribe headings in an illuminated manuscript; the practice dates back to medieval Europe, where trained rubricators added red headings and characters to separate or emphasize sections of text

rump par•ty /rəmp pär′-tē/ ***n.*** in Great Britain, members of a political party left behind after the party suffers a breakup or dissolution

sack•but /sak′-bət/ ***n.*** [From the Middle French words *sacquer* and *bouter*, meaning “to push” and “to pull”] a Renaissance sliding horn strongly resembling a trombone

salt•pe•ter /sôlt-pē′-tər/ ***n.*** an alternative name for the chemical potassium nitrate

Sap•phic stan•za /sa′-fik stan′-zə/ ***n.*** a poetic form of four lines invented by the Greek poet Sappho

sauce•box /sôs′-bäks/ ***n.*** an impudent, back-talking person, particularly a child

sax /saks/ ***n.*** a colloquial term for a saxophone, a woodwind instrument

Schwann's white sub•stance /shwänz wīt səb′-stən(t)s/ ***n.*** in human anatomy, a material found in the medullary sheath or myelin sheath, the insulating sac that surrounds human nerve-cell fibers; the material is 80 percent fat, giving it a whitish appearance <***Schwann's white substance*** is named after the man who discovered it, the seminal German physiologist and cytologist Theodor Schwann (1810–1882).>

screw•cap /skrü′-kap/ ***n.*** a metal alternative to a cork to keep a wine bottle sealed

screw head /skrü hed/ ***n.*** the top of a metal screw, which engages the screwdriver

screw jack /skrü jak/ ***n.*** a hand-cranked or a hydraulic device used to raise objects several feet or several yards into the air; ***also known as*** jackscrew <The threaded rod of the ***screw jack*** turns through a nut, held by movable metal bars connected to a metal plate, which effectively raises heavy loads such as cars and trucks.>

screw ma•chine /skrü mə′-shēn/ ***n.*** a metalworking machine used to make turned components

scut•tle•butt /skə′-təl-bət/ ***n.*** the freshwater barrel on sailing ships where sailors gather to converse

sea cock /sē käk/ ***n.*** a valve on a steamship that carefully controls any intake of ocean water

sea•men /sē′-mən/ ***n.*** two or more sailors

sects /seks/ ***n.*** small religious groups with their own religious doctrines

seer•suck•er /sir′-sə-kər/ ***n.*** a type of light, crinkled linen or other cloth

sekts /seks/ ***n.*** German sparkling wines

SEX ***abbr.*** the acronym for the chemical compound sodium ethyl xanthate

sex•a•ge•nar•i•an /sek-sə-jə-ner′-ē-ən/ ***n.*** an elderly person, male or female, in the sixth decade of life, that is, between sixty and sixty-nine years old

sex•a•ges•i•ma /sek-sə-je′-sə-mə/ ***n.*** in the Catholic religion, the second Sunday before Ash Wednesday

sex•i•thi•o•phene /sek-si-thī′-ə-fēn/ ***n.*** a molecule with six subunits of thiophene rings

sex link•age /seks link′-ij/ ***n.*** the inheritance of a sex chromosome as linked to a given gene

sex•tant /seks′-tənt/ ***n.*** a common navigational instrument on ships

sex•tet /seks-tet′/ ***n.*** any group containing six people

sex•tup•lets /seks-tə′-pləts/ ***n.*** six identical babies, all born at roughly the same time

sex•us /sek′-səs/ ***n.*** a person's biological gender, that is, male or female

shii•ta•ke /shē-tä′-kē/ ***n.*** a nonpoisonous edible Asian mushroom

shite /shtē/ ***n.*** the lead actor in Japanese Noh theatre

shit•tah /shi′-tə/ ***n.*** an Asian acacia tree (*Acacia albida*) mentioned in the Old Testament; still flourishes in Jordan and in the Sinai Peninsula region of Egypt <The wood of the ***shittah*** tree is called shittim and was used by the ancient Jewish people to construct the Ark of the Covenant, the sacred vessel for the Tabernacle of Moses.>

> "I will plant in the wilderness the cedar, the shittah tree, and the myrtle, and the oil tree; I will set in the desert the fir tree, the pine, and the box tree together: That they may see, and know, and consider, and understand together, that the hand of the Lord hath done this, and the Holy One of Israel hath created it."
>
> —Isaiah, 41:19–20.

shit•tim•wood /shi′-təm-wûd/ ***n.*** the wood from the shittah tree

shut•tle•cock /shə-təl-käk′/ ***n.*** in badminton, a piece of cork, with feathers attached, hit over a net to score points

sil•i•cone balls /si′-lə-kōn bôlz/ ***n.*** the smooth bouncing objects used in juggling

sin bin /sin bin/ ***n.*** in hockey, a colloquial term for the penalty box where rule-breaking players sit

skin div•er /skin dī′-vər/ ***n.*** one who swims deep underwater while wearing breathing apparatus

slime•head /slīm′-hed/ ***n.*** a small, long-lived, deep-sea fish

slip•pery dick /sli′-pə-rē dik/ ***n.*** a saltwater fish (*Halichoeres bivittatus*) of the family Labridae that lives in coral reefs and shallow sandbars throughout the Atlantic Ocean, in a region extending from North Carolina to South America <A mature ***slippery dick*** can grow to an impressive nine inches long.>

smeg•mat•ic /smeg-ma′-tik/ ***adj.*** soapy; having to do with soap

snatch block /snach bläk/ ***n.*** a single- or multiple-pulley assembly in which the block's eye can be opened along a hinge to insert a line, either a rope or a metal cable

sod•am•ide /sō′-də-mīd/ ***n.*** the chemical sodium amide

sod•dy•ite /sä′-dē-īt/ ***n.*** a mineral named for British physicist and chemist Frederick Soddy (1877–1956)

spank•er /spaŋ′-kər/ ***n.*** a specific type of canvas sail used on a large, three-masted sailing ship

spanker

spas•mod•ic po•ets /spaz-mä′-dik pō′-əts/ ***n.*** a group of British poets writing during the Victorian era

sper•ma•ce•ti /spər-mə-sē′-tē/ ***n.*** the white oil found in the head of a sperm whale

Sper•mo /spər′-mō/ ***n.*** the Greek goddess of grain

sperm•o•phile /spər′-mə-fīl/ ***n.*** a rodent resembling a squirrel that inhabits subterranean burrows

sperm whale /spərm wāl/ ***n.*** a large whale (*Physeter macrocephalus*) having teeth instead of strandlike baleen <The ***sperm whale*** can grow up to sixty feet long, with a massive head and huge conical teeth in its lower jaw.>

> "I tell you, the sperm whale will stand no nonsense."
>
> —HERMAN MELVILLE, *MOBY DICK*

spon•ta•ne•ous em•is•sion /span-tā-nē-əs ē-mi′-shən/ ***n.*** the process by which an electron, a subatomic particle, decays to a lower energy state

spot•ted dick /spä′-təd dik/ ***n.*** a traditional British dessert pudding served with thick, steaming-hot custard; ***also known as*** spotted dog <***Spotted dick*** is usually made with flour, milk, butter, white or brown sugar, and dried fruit such as currants. The word *spotted* refers to the dotlike currants in the pudding, while *dick* may refer to the dough.>

squeeze box /skwēz bäks/ ***n.*** a portable box-shaped musical instrument

squeeze off /skwēz ôf/ ***vb.*** to fire rounds from a firearm, usually a handgun

stic•ky dog /sti′-kē dôg/ ***n.*** a drying wicket in the game of cricket that is difficult to bat on

stiff•nut /stif′-nət/ ***n.*** an alternative term for a lock nut

stim•u•lat•ed em•is•sion /stim′-yə-lā-təd ē-mi′-shən/ ***n.*** a phenomenon in physics during which an electron, or negatively charged subatomic particle, is hit with a photon, or discrete particle of light energy, causing the electron to emit a photon; ***also called*** optical amplification <***Stimulated emission*** makes possible lasers, or devices that project coherent light beams; in fact, the word *laser* is an acronym for "light amplification by stimulated emission of radiation.">

stud mas•ter /stəd mas′-tər/ ***n.*** a person who oversees the breeding stock of a horse owner

studs /stəds/ ***n.*** the smaller vertical wood beams used in home construction

stuff•ing balls /stə′-fiŋ bôlz/ ***n.*** baked or fried balls of stuffing mixture, generally made of breadcrumbs, diced onion, sausage meat, and spices such as sage, pepper, and salt <***Stuffing balls*** can be placed in turkeys and other fowl or meats as a substitute for loose stuffing mixture.>

stuff•ing box /stə′-fiŋ bäks/ ***n.*** the sealed area around a propeller shaft where the shaft exits a boat

suc•cor /sə′-kər/ ***vb.*** to help someone during hard times

suc•co•tash /sə′-kə-tash/ ***n.*** a stew made of lima beans and corn

suc•cu•bus /sə′-kyə-bəs/ ***n.*** according to ancient Mesopotamian beliefs, a female demon who wended her way into men's dreams and drained away their life force

suck•er /sə′-kər/ ***n.*** a budding shoot near a tree base

suck•er hole /sə′-kər hōl/ ***n.*** a sailor's term for a short period of seemingly good weather

suck•ing pig /sə′-kiŋ pig/ ***n.*** an alternative term for a suckling pig that has fed only on its mother's milk

suck re•flex /sək rē′-fleks/ ***n.*** the natural reflex of most human babies to put things in their mouths and repeatedly suck on them; common sucking objects are fingers, toes, and baby bottles

sweet spot /swēt spät/ ***n.*** the area on the face of a cricket bat that provides maximum power

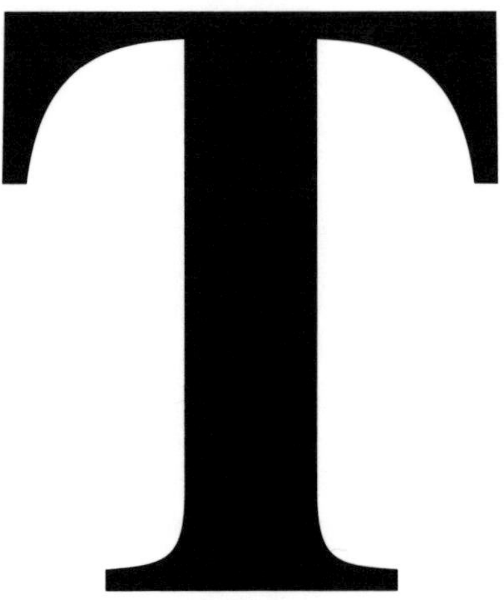

tail slide /tāl slīd/ ***n.*** a slide performed on the tail, or upturned end of a skateboard

tes•ta•ceous /tes-tā′-shəs/ ***adj.*** covered with a shell

tes•ty /tes′-tē/ ***n.*** impatient, irritated, exasperated

thes•pi•an /thes′-pē-ən/ ***n.*** an actor or actress

tight end /tīt end/ ***n.*** a player in American football whose position varies according to the instructions of the coach <The ***tight end***, who may be an offensive lineman, wide receiver, etc., receives passes from the quarterback or prevents other players from tackling the player carrying the ball. Perhaps the greatest tight end in football history is

Mike Ditka, whose 427 receptions and 43 touchdowns with the Chicago Bears and other teams garnered him an induction into the Football Hall of Fame in 1988.>

tit•bit /tit′-bit/ ***n.*** the British way of spelling ***tidbit***, a nice bit of food, gossip, or exciting news

tit for tat /tit fər tat/ ***n.*** an equivalent response

ti•ti /ti′-tē/ ***n.*** a type of monkey native to South America

tit•mouse /tit′-maûs/ ***n.*** a small songbird with gray feathers and a large crest

ti•tra•tion /tī-trā′-shən/ ***n.*** in medicine, the act of gradually adjusting the dose of a medication

tit•ter /tit′-ər/ ***vb.*** to laugh in a silly, insecure manner

to•fu balls /tō′-fü bôlz/ ***n.*** in Asian coking, baked balls of tofu and seasonings that are eaten with rice

tongue and groove /təŋ ənd grüv/ ***n.*** a type of wood siding in which the projecting edge of one board fits into a channel in the next

touch•hole /təch′-hōl/ ***n.*** a hole in the rear of a cannon that is used to ignite an explosive charge

touchhole

trip•le lay /trip′-əl lā/ ***n.*** in firefighting, a method of loading a fire hose

tur•duck•en /tər′-dək-ən/ ***n.*** a chicken stuffed in a duck, which is then stuffed in a turkey; the whole is then barbecued

tur•dus /tərd′-əs/ ***n.*** a genus of birds known as true thrushes

twat•tle /twa′-tᵊl/ ***n.*** silly, worthless talk

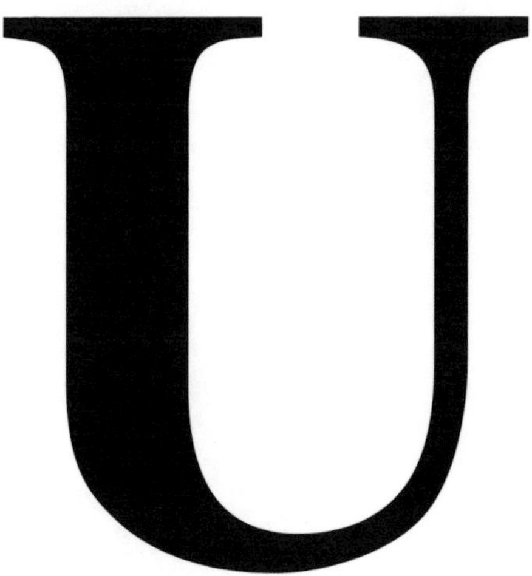

up and in /əp ənd in/ ***n.*** the term for a stock option that activates as soon as share prices rise in trading

up•com•ing /əp-kəm′-iŋ/ ***adj.*** arriving soon; forthcoming

U•ra•nus /yûr′-əh-nəs ***or*** yûr-ā′-nəs/ ***n.*** the seventh planet from the sun

ur•i•nat•or /yûr′-i-nā-tər/ ***n.*** [From the Latin word *urinari*, meaning "to plunge" or "to dive underwater"] a person who searches for underwater riches; for example, a pearl diver

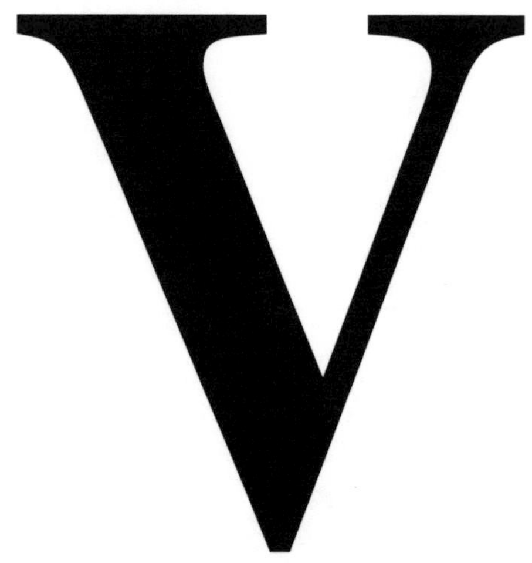

va•gi•na gen•ti•um /və-jī′-nə jen′-tē-əm/ ***n.*** [A Latin phrase meaning "the womb of all nations"] in anthropology, the reputed prehistoric birthplace of modern humans <Based on available fossil evidence, the ***vagina gentium*** is undoubtedly the continent of Africa, probably in Ethiopia.>

vag•i•na•ta vir•ga•ta /vaj-i-nä′-tə vir-gä′-tə/ ***n.*** a species of edible mushroom cultivated throughout Asia

vag•i•nate /vaj′-ə-nət/ ***adj.*** sheathed; secured in a sheath or scabbard

vag•i•nic•o•la /vaj-i-nə-kō′-lə/ ***n.*** the genus *Infusoria*, or microorganisms often found in rotting organic material

ver•gence /vər′-jən(t)s/ ***n.*** the simultaneous movement of both eyes in opposite directions

vergence

vi•bra•to /vi-brä′-tō/ ***n.*** a pulsating musical effect; ***also***, a wavering of tone while singing

vi•bro•tac•tile aids /vī-brō-tak′-tīl ādz/ ***n.*** tiny battery-powered devices attached to a deaf person's body that change sounds into radio signals then transmitted to the user's skin, allowing the person to feel the vibration of sounds

vir•gin wool /vər′-jən wûl/ ***n.*** a sheep's wool that has been spun for the first time

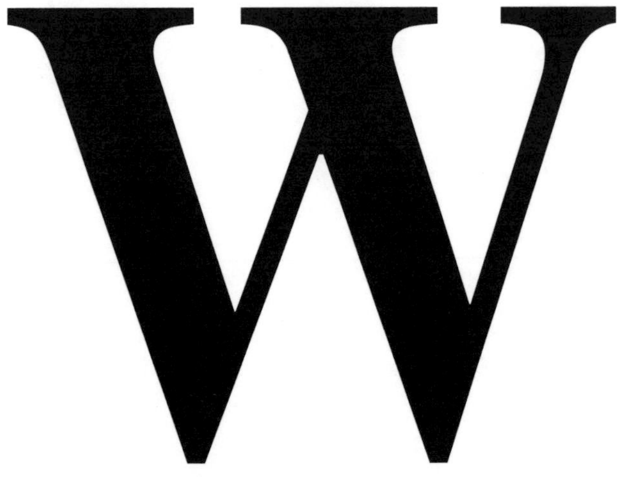

wa•ter cock /wôt′-tər käk/ ***n.*** an Australian bird; the male of the species has a fleshy red horn on its head

wet nurse /wet nərs/ ***n.*** a woman hired to breast-feed another woman's baby

white ball /wīt bôl/ ***n.*** an alternate name for the cue ball in the games of pool or snooker

white-breast•ed nut•hatch /wīt′-bres-təd nət′-hach/ ***n.*** a small North American songbird (*Sitta carolinensis*) with black and blue-gray feathers and a white-feathered face <The ***white-breasted nuthatch*** emits a distinctive "Yeah, yeah, yeah!" song as it hangs upside down in trees.>

white•face clown /wīt′-fās klaûn/ ***n.*** a circus clown performing in whiteface makeup

white hole /wīt hōl′/ ***n.*** in astrophysics, a celestial body that ejects matter (as opposed to a black hole, which pulls matter inward)

white hore•hound /wīt hōr′-haûnd/ ***n.*** a perennial flowering plant in the family Lamiaceae

white sauce /wīt sôs/ ***n.*** a sauce for vegetables that is made of butter, milk, and seasonings

wo•man of the bed•cham•ber /wû′-mən əv thə bed′-chām-bər/ ***n.*** in Great Britain, a woman who is a servant to a Queen Regnant or a Queen Consort

wood•cock /wûd′-käk/ ***n.*** a bird of the genus *Scolopax* having brown or black feathers

wool•ly butt /wûl′-ē bət/ ***n.*** a fast-growing tree (*Eucalyptus longifolia*) found primarily in the state of New South Wales, in southeastern Australia, that produces greenish gray leaves and white blooms and is covered with a furry bark resembling wool

woolly butt

wor•ry balls /wər′-ē bôlz/ ***n.*** Chinese meditation orbs that are manipulated by hand to induce calmness

X
YZ

XO sex-de•ter•mi•na•tion sys•tem /eks-ō seks-dē-tərm-i-nā′-shən sis′-təm/ ***n.*** a process used by certain insects to determine the offspring's gender

X-ring /eks′-riŋ/ ***n.*** the famed brass graduation ring awarded to graduates in good standing of the St. Francis Xavier University <The ***X-ring*** features a large X and is so highly prized by St. Francis's alumnae that it has become the school's official emblem.>

XXX /eks-eks-eks/ ***n.*** the number thirty written in Roman numerals

yarn bra /yarn brä/ ***n.*** a mesh pouch for holding a ball of yarn while knitting

yel•low boy /yel′-ō boi/ ***n.*** a British gold coin <An example of a ***yellow boy*** is the guinea, the first machine-minted gold coin produced by the British Empire; it was worth one pound sterling, or twenty shillings, although that value often increased due to fluctuations in the price of gold.>

yellow boy

yel•low leg mush•room /yel′-ō leg məsh′-rüm/ ***n.*** a common mushroom that grows in wooded areas and damp places

zad•dick /tsäd′-ik/ ***n.*** a just and righteous man in the Jewish religion

Zam•bo•ni /zam-bō′-nē/ ***n.*** a mechanized vehicle for smoothing ice at hockey games

zax /zaks/ ***n.*** a tool used for trimming roof slates

zone of elon•ga•tion /zōn əf ē-lôŋ-gā′-shən/ ***n.*** the area in plant roots where cells grow and enlarge

Beaver Lick & Bitchfield

A Glossary of Tragically Misunderstood Places

As•sa•wo•man /as-ə-wō′-mən/ a community in Accomack County, Virginia, that is not formally incorporated as a self-governing town but is chiefly administered by Accomack County

Asse /ä′-sə/ a municipality in Lower Saxony, Germany

Balls•bridge /bôlz′-brij/ a suburb of Dublin, Ireland

Barf /bärf/ a mountainous region in the Lake District of Cumbria, England, that borders Bassenthwaite Lake, the largest of the district's sixteen lakes

Bås•tad /bôsh′-stôd/ a municipality in Scania, Sweden

Bas•tar /bäs′-tär/ a state in India

Beav•er /bē′-vər/ a village in northeastern Alaska

Beav•er•lick /bē′-vər-lik/ a city in Boone County, Kentucky

Big Bone Lick State Park /big bōn lik stāt pärk/ a state park near the town of Big Bone, in Boone County, Kentucky <The word *lick* in the park's name refers to the fact that wild animals gather there to lick the abundant salt found in the park's soil and springs.>

Big Hole Riv•er /big hōl ri′-vər/ a tributary of the Jefferson River in Montana

Bitch•field /bich′-fēld/ a tiny village in Lincolnshire, England <The village's main street, Dark Lane, separates the two parts of ***Bitchfield***, known as Lower Bitchfield and Bitchfield.>

Boo•ti Boo•ti Na•tion•al Park /bü′-tē bü′-tē nash′-nəl pärk/ a national park in New South Wales, Australia

Brest /brest/ a seaport in the Finistère area of France

Buck•head /bək′-hed/ a village in the northern section of Atlanta, Georgia

Bull•skin /bəl′-skin/ a township in Fayette County, Pennsylvania

Bun•gay /bən′-gā/ a town in Suffolk, England

Butt Bridge /bət brij/ A bridge and roadway over the River Liffey in Dublin, Ireland

Butte /byüt/ a city in Silver Bow County, Montana

Butt of Lew•is /bət əv lü′-is/ the northernmost point of the isle of Lewis, Scotland

Butz•town /bətz′-taûn/ a city in Northampton County, Pennsylvania

Cape Cir•cum•ci•sion /cāp sər-kəm-si′-zhən/ a peninsula on Bouvet Island, a sub-Antarctic island discovered by the French explorer Jean-Baptiste Charles Bouvet de Lozier on January 1, 1739 <Because the Catholic holiday known as the Feast of the Circumcision also falls on January 1, Bouvet named his new peninsula ***Cape Circumcision***.>

Cel•lar•dyke /sel′-ər-dīk/ a village in Fife, Scotland

Cli•max Springs /klī′-maks spriŋz/ a village in Camden County, Missouri

Clit /klēt/ a village in Arad County, Romania

Cock•er•mouth /kä′-kər-maûth/ a picturesque town in Great Britain, in the Lake District of Cumbria, England, near the Cocker and Derwent rivers <***Cockermouth*** is internationally famous as the birthplace of the renowned British Romantic poet William Wordsworth.>

Cock•er Riv•er /käk′-ər ri′-vər/ a river in Cumbria County, England

Cock•ing /kä′-kiŋ/ a village and civil parish in West Sussex, England

Con•dom /kōn-dōm′/ a town in Gers, France

Cox•hoe /käks′-hō/ a village in the County of Durham, England.

Cox•sack•ie /kûk-säk′-ē/ a town in Greene County, New York

Cum•ming /kəm′-iŋ/ a city in Forsyth County, Georgia

Cum•mings Park /kəm′-iŋz pärk/ a park located in Stamford, Connecticut

Cum•ming Street /kəm′-iŋ strēt/ a street that intersects Seaman Avenue in the Inwood area of upper New York City <***Cumming Street*** can be reached by traveling west on Dyckman Street and turning right onto Seaman.>

Cunt•er /kün′-tər/ a village in the Albula district of Switzerland

Dev•il's Dyke /dev′-əlz dīk/ a valley on the South Downs Way in England

Dev•il's Wa•ter /dev′-əlz wôt′-ər/ a river near Hexham in Northumberland, England

Did•ling /did′-liŋ/ a hamlet in West Sussex, England

Dil•do /dil′-dō/ a small seaside town in Newfoundland, Canada

Diss /dis/ a town in Norfolk, England

Duck•hole /dək′-hōl/ a small village in south Gloucestershire, England

Dyke /dīk/ a hamlet in Lincolnshire, England

Fair Head /fer hed/ a rocky headland in Northern Ireland

Fan•ny /fan′-ē/ a community in Wyoming County, West Virginia

Fan•ny Bay /fan′-ē bā/ a village in British Columbia, Canada

Far•town /fär′-taûn/ a suburb of Huddersfield, in west Yorkshire County, England

Fing•ring•hoe /fiŋ′-griŋ-hō/ a village and civil parish near Colchester, England.

Flush•ing /fləsh′-iŋ/ a neighborhood in the borough of Queens, in New York City

Foul•ness /faûl′-nəs/ an island on the east coast of Essex, England

French Lick /french lik/ a town in Orange County, Indiana

Frog But•tress /frôg bə′-trəs/ a rock-climbing area near the town of Boonah, Australia

Fuck•ing /fü′-kiŋ/ a village of about 150 people in the municipality of Tarsdorf, in the Innvietel region of upper Austria, near the border with Bavaria, Germany <The name ***Fucking*** comes from an early eleventh-century founder named Focko and means "the Place of Focko's People.">

Fuk•i•en /fü′-kē-en/ a province on the Taiwan Strait in southeastern China

Gas /gas/ a city in Allen County, Kansas

Gass•ville /gas′-vil/ a city in Baxter, Arkansas

Gay /gā/ a town in Meriwether County, Georgia

Gay Head /gā hed/ a town on the island of Martha's Vineyard, Massachusetts <Founded in 1699 by English settlers and incorporated in 1870, ***Gay Head*** was purportedly named after the island's gaily colored cliffs. In 1997 residents decided to restore the town's original Native American name, Aquinnah.>

Gays /gāz/ a village in Moultrie County, Illinois

Gay•ville /gā′-vil/ a town in Yankton County, South Dakota

Glass•cock /glas′-käk/ a county in west-central Texas

Grab•hair /grä′-vēr/ a village on the shore of Loch Oldhairn in Scotland

Green•head /grēn′-hed/ a small village in Northumberland, England

Grosse Tête /grōs tet/ a village in Iberville Parish, Louisiana

Hard•en /hard′-ən/ a township in New South Wales, Australia

Hell Cor•ner /hel kôr′-nər/ a village in Berkshire, England

Hell Hole Gorge /hel hōl gôrj/ a national park in Queensland, Australia

High Dyke /hī dīk/ a village in County Durham, England

Horn•dean /hôrn′-dēn/ a village and civil parish in Hampshire, England

Horn•ing /hôrn′-iŋ/ an ancient village in Norfolk, England

Hor•pit /hōr′-pit/ an agricultural hamlet in Wiltshire County, England

Hose /hōz/ a village in Leicestershire County, England

In•ter•course /in′-tər-kôrs/ a village in Lancaster County, Pennsylvania

Jack•field /jak′-fēld/ a village in the Ironbridge Gorge, Shropshire, England

Kies•ter /kēs′-tər/ a city in Faribault County, Minnesota

Knock•in /nôk′-in/ a village and civil parish in Shropshire, England

Kra•bi /krä′-bē/ a southern province in Thailand

La•go de Poo•pó /lä′-gō dā pü′-pō/ a lake in western Bolivia

Lake Ni•piss•ing /lāk ni-pis′-iŋ/ the fifth-largest lake in Ontario, Canada

Lake Ti•ti•ca•ca /lāk ti-tē-kä′-kä/ Earth's highest navigable lake, approximately 13,000 feet above sea level <*Lake Titicaca* is located between Bolivia and Peru and is owned jointly by the two countries. Water flows from the lake into the Desaguadero River and from there to Bolivia's Lake Poopó.>

Le Tam•pon /lə tam-pōn′/ a commune on the French island of Réunion

Lick•ey End /lik′-ē end/ a village and civil parish in Worcestershire, England

Lick•ing /lik′-iŋ/ a city in Texas County, Missouri

Love Can•al /ləv kə-nal′/ a community in Niagara Falls, New York

Love•land /ləv′-land/ a city in Larimer County, Colorado

Low•er Bitch•field /lō′-ər bich′-fēld/ part of the village of Bitchfield, in Lincolnshire, England

Low•er Toot•ing /lō′-ər tü′-tiŋ/ a neighborhood in London, England

Mas•bate /môs-bä′-tē/ one of the Philippine Islands

May•bush /mā′-bəsh/ a district in Southampton, England

Mens•trie /men′-strē/ a village in the Clackmannanshire region of Scotland

Meth•lick /meth′-lik/ a village in Aberdeenshire, Scotland

Mid•del•fart /mil′-fär/ a town on the island of Funen, part of Denmark. <***Middelfart*** means "Middle Passage," a reference to a well-used waterway connecting Funen with Jutland Peninsula on the mainland. The town is noted for its beautiful seacoast and downtown cultural center.>

Moor•head /mōr′-hed/ a city in Monona County, Iowa

More•head Ci•ty /mōr′-hed sit′-ē/ a city on the seacoast of North Carolina

Mount•joy /maûnt′-joi/ a village in County Tyrone, Northern Ireland

Mount Tit•lis /maûnt tit′-lis/ a ten-thousand-foot-high snow-covered mountain in the Swiss Alps, in Obwalden, near Bern, Switzerland

Nas•ty /nas′-tē/ a village in Hertfordshire, England

North Bitch•burn /nôrth bich′-bərn/ a village in County Durham, England

North Cock•er•ing•ton /nôrth käk-riŋ′-tən/ a village in Lincolnshire County, England

Nut•bush /nət′-büsh/ a farming community in western Tennessee

Nut•field /nət′-fēld/ a suburb of Melbourne, Australia

Old Leake /ōld lēk/ a village in Lincolnshire, England

Pee Pee Town•ship /pē pē taûn′-ship/ A civil township founded in 1798 in Pike County, Ohio. <***Pee Pee Township*** covers about thirty-two square miles and has a population of about eight thousand residents, according to the 2000 census. The township's name purportedly comes from the initials of an early Irish pioneer.>

Pen•ile /pē′-nīl/ a neighborhood in Louisville, Kentucky

Pen•is•ar•wain /pe-nis-ər-wān′/ a village near Caernarfon in Gwynedd, Wales

Pen•is•tone /pen′-i-stən/ a market town in south Yorkshire, England

Pe•ter•head /pēt′-ər-hed/ a town in Aberdeenshire, Scotland

Phuck•et /fü-ket′/ a large resort island off the southwestern coast of Thailand

Pis•sa Riv•er /pis′-ə ri′-vər/ a river in Kaliningrad Oblast, in northwestern Russia

Pratt's Bot•tom /prats bä′-təm/ a village in the borough of Bromley, London, England

Pump Gey•ser /pəmp gī′-zər/ a steam geyser in Yellowstone National Park

Pus•sy /pü-sē′/ a village in Savoie, France

Queens•town /kwēnz′-taûn/ a city in Australia

Queens•ville /kwēnz′-vil/ a village in Ontario, Canada

Rams•bot•tom /ramz′-bä-təm/ a town in greater Manchester, England

San•dy Balls /san′-dē bôlz/ a resort area in New Forest Hampshire, in England

Sexi /sesh′-ē/ an ancient Phoenician colony in present-day Spain

Sex•mo•an /seks′-mō-än/ a city in the province of Pampanga, the Philippines

Shag Har•bour /shag här′-bər/ a small fishing village in Nova Scotia, Canada

Shit•ter•ton /shi′-tər-tən/ a hamlet in the Purbeck district of Dorset, England

Suck•ley /sək′-lē/ a village in Worcestershire, England

Suck Riv•er /sək ri′-vər/ the main tributary of the Shannon River, in Ireland

Tittes•worth Res•er•voir /tits′-wərth rez′-əv-wär/ a water-storage reservoir in Staffordshire, England

Tit•ty•bong /ti′-tē-bôŋ/ a small agricultural community in the Australian state of Victoria

Tong Fuk /tôŋ fük/ a resort village near Hong Kong, China

Tongue /təŋ/ a coastal village in Highland, Scotland

Twatt /twat/ a village in the Shetland Islands, Scotland

Undy /ən′-dē/ a village in Monmouthshire, Wales

Up•per Dick•er /əp′-ər di′-kər/ a village in East Sussex, England

Up•per•thong /əp′-ər-thôŋ/ a village in west Yorkshire, England

Vir•gin /vər′-jən/ a town in Washington County, Utah

Wac•ker•field /wa′-kər-fēld/ a village in County Durham, England

Wa•ter of Ken /wôt′-ər əv ken/ a river in Galloway, in southwestern Scotland

We•cock /wē′-käk/ a council estate on the edges of Waterlooville, England

Wei•ner /wē′-nər/ a city in Poinsett County, Arkansas

Wet•wang /wet′-waŋ/ a village in the Yorkshire Wolds, England

Whore•house Mead•ows /hōr′-haûs med′-ōz/ an area in the Steens Mountains near Frenchglen, Oregon

Yung-ho /yüŋ-hō′/ a city in Taipei County, Taiwan